THE SCANDALOUS MESSAGE
OF JAMES

If a brother or sister is ill-clad
and in lack of daily food,
and one of you says to them,
"Go in peace, be warmed and filled,"
without giving them the things needed for the body,
what does it profit?
So faith by itself, if it has no works, is dead.
But some one will say,
"You have faith and I have works."
Show me your faith apart from works,
and I by my works will show you my faith. . . .
For as the body without the spirit is dead,
so faith without works is dead.

—*James 2:15–18, 26,* RSV

THE SCANDALOUS MESSAGE
OF JAMES

Faith Without Works Is Dead

ELSA TAMEZ

90

A Meyer-Stone Book

CROSSROAD • NEW YORK

To Lucila and Carlos, my parents

1990

The Crossroad Publishing Company
370 Lexington Avenue, New York, NY 10017

Translated by John Eagleson
Scripture quotations are from the Jerusalem Bible © 1966 by Darton,
Longman & Todd, Ltd. and Doubleday & Company, Inc.

First presented at the Facultad Metodista de Teología, São Paulo, Brazil,
for the Semana Teológica Wesleyana, May 1985.
First published as *Santiago: Lectura latinoamericana de la epístola*,
by Editorial DEI, Apartado Postal 390–2070 Sabanilla, San José, Costa Rica.
© 1985 by Departamento Ecuménico de Investigaciones and Elsa Tamez.
English translation © 1990 by the Crossroad Publishing Company

Printed in the United States of America
94 93 92 91 90   5 4 3 2 1

Library of Congress Cataloging in Publication Data
Tamez, Elsa.
    [Santiago. English]
    The scandalous message of James : faith without works is dead /
Elsa Tamez ; [translated by John Eagleson].
    p. cm.
    Translation of: Santiago.
    Bibliography: p.
    Includes index.
    ISBN 0-940989-56-5
    1. Bible. N.T. James — Criticism, interpretation, etc.
2. Christianity and justice — Biblical teaching.   3. Latin America —
Church history — 20th century.   I. Title.
BS2785.6.J8T3513   1989
227'.9106 — dc20   89-40239
                                                         CIP

Contents

Foreword

Elsa Tamez, the young Mexican theologian and professor at the Latin American Biblical Seminary in Costa Rica, the author of *Bible of the Oppressed* and *Against Machismo*, has struck again! This fresh and original commentary on the Epistle of James, the forgotten, skipped over, and despised letter to Christian communities in the first century, comes alive for Christian communities suffering oppression, marginalization, and even persecution in Latin America and elsewhere, and now, through its English translation, it comes alive for the socially mixed Christian communities in North America.

The author brings with her, not only her scholarship and clever use of the Greek of the New Testament and her particular perspective as a Latin American and a woman theologian, but also her unique gift of literary reading, re-reading, and communicating. It is serious exegetical work, letting the text speak for itself, and the context to take shape through the text itself, and all of that enhanced by the simple and clarifying devises of reading back and forth, looking now from one angle and then from another, sorting out a thread or weaving through passages and concepts, letting the words shine forth in all their power and nuances, in pure Jamesian style: "listen!" "behold!"

Elsa Tamez reminds us that James was an "open letter" but it would be an "intercepted letter" by some governments of our day, because of its subversive potential for what it says on the rich and the poor. Actually, it has been an intercepted letter many times through history by Christians and churches themselves, during the canon processes in the first centuries, despised by Luther during the theological warfare of the Reformation times, skipped from liturgies in congregations of the rich, put aside by theologians for supposed "theological reductionism," or minimized for its paraenetic character in our "logocentric societies."

But thanks to Elsa Tamez's creative work it can become again "an open letter" for strong Christians called through this letter to daring hope, working faith, "militant patience," and praxis with integrity. This letter and this commentary are meant to bring on a crisis for us, and an option: intercepted letter or open letter?

—MORTIMER ARIAS

Chapter 1

The Intercepted Letter

IF THE LETTER OF JAMES were sent to the Christian communities of Latin America today, it would very possibly be intercepted by the National Security governments in certain countries. The document would be branded as subversive because of the paragraphs that vehemently denounce the exploitation by landowners (5:1–6) and the carefree life of the merchants (4:13–17). The passage that affirms that "pure, unspoilt religion, in the eyes of God our Father is this: coming to the help of orphans and widows when they need it, and keeping oneself uncontaminated by the world" (1:27) would be criticized as "reductionism" of the gospel or as Marxist-Leninist infiltration in the churches. The communities to which the letter was addressed would become very suspicious to the authorities.

But I am speaking of a very ancient letter written by a man named James to the first Christian churches. We are dealing with a servant of Jesus Christ concerned with the poor and oppressed people of his times, people who were undergoing unbearable suffering and were in need of strength and hope. James offered them a word of encouragement and advice.

Attempts at "Interception" Throughout History

Reading the history of this document (similar to that of other documents, although this has been more consistently disparaged than many), we realize that there is something in the letter that has made church authorities regard it with suspicion. Although the letter was probably written at the end of the first century or the beginning of the second, it was not finally accepted as part of the canon until the end of the fourth century, and in some churches it continued to be questioned in subsequent centuries.[1]

Challenges to the letter did not end after the formation of the canon. At the beginning of the sixteenth century (1516) Erasmus, in his *Annotationes* to the first printed edition of the Greek New Testament, again mentions the problems surrounding the canonical recognition of the letter. Referring to the language and style of the letter, he added his own doubts regarding its apostolic authorship.

A few years after Erasmus, the letter suffered the most ferocious attacks at the hands of Martin Luther. Who doesn't recall the famous phrase "the epistle of straw" on hearing the name of James? Unfortunately, on a popular level the best known commentaries on James are those of Luther.

Luther could not accept the Letter of James, nor could he accept Hebrews, Jude, or Revelation. But it was the

Letter of James that he most disdained. For him the letter was not faithful to the gospel of Christ, namely, according to Luther, the doctrine of salvation by faith. In his preface to the first edition to the New Testament, he asserts:

> St. John's Gospel and his first epistle, St. Paul's epistles, especially Romans, Galatians, and Ephesians, and St. Peter's first epistle are the books that show you Christ and teach you all that is necessary and salvatory for you to know, even if you were never to see or hear any other book or doctrine. Therefore St. James' epistle is really an epistle of straw, compared to these others, for it has nothing of the nature of the gospel about it.[2]

Luther placed the books of James, Hebrews, Jude, and Revelation at the end of his German translation of the New Testament, but he assigned them no numbers in his table of contents. The modern edition of Luther's translation of the German Bible still puts these books at the end of the New Testament — but they are included in the table of contents. The disdain for the letter continued. So, for example, according to Donald Guthrie, nineteenth-century biblical criticism considered the letter to be a product of a brand of Christianity inferior to Pauline theology.[3]

We wonder why there were so many "buts" involved before the letter was recognized as a part of the gospel message. The reasons are various and of very different nature. Apostolic authorship was one of the most important criteria used by the early church to determine a document's inclusion in the canon. The letters of Paul and the Gospels were quickly included. Because of uncertain authorship, others took longer. The Letter of James was a candidate from the beginning. But it was often questioned whether the author was James the brother of the Lord.

Why did the letter come to be known so late? Some believe that originally the letter did not carry the name of James, and so it was considered unimportant; but there is no basis for such an affirmation. Dibelius believes that the lack of mention has to do with the paraenetic character of the letter. He says that a document of moral exhortations is relevant at a certain time and for certain circumstances, and later such exhortations became obsolete. But when James was recognized as the brother of the Lord, the document was reevaluated.[4]

As we read the central message of James, though, we wonder when a document that defends the oppressed from injustice becomes irrelevant. For there have always been oppressed people.

Another of the objections to the letter is that there is little mention of Jesus, or little Christology. But is it not James who makes most mention of the sayings of Jesus? The Sermon on the Mount appears almost in its entirety in the letter.[5] Why should we give importance to what is said about Jesus and not to what Jesus said?

In Luther's case it is clear that the Letter of James did not fit into his doctrine of justification by faith alone. Using the very words of Paul, although with a different meaning as we shall see, James asserts that faith without works is dead, and that a person is justified by works and not only by faith (2:24). We should not level anachronistic criticisms at Luther, nor assert that he totally rejected the letter. Luther recognizes that it was written by a pious man (according to him, the son of Zebedee). He accepts its position on the law of God, but he does not give it apostolic authority. As he says: "I will not have it in my Bible in the number of the proper chief books, but do not intend thereby to forbid anyone to place and exalt it as he pleases, for there is many a good saying in it."[6] Nevertheless, we have to recognize that his comments have been in large part responsible for the secondary position of the letter today.

This is a letter that seems important for us to recover and re-read in Latin America. Notwithstanding all its difficulties, the letter was not "intercepted." It has survived, thanks to its defenders throughout Christian history and to the Holy Spirit. Today nobody doubts its authenticity as part of our canon.

Still, although it might seem strange, we can say that the attempts at unconscious "interception" still continue. For example:

a. There is a surprising dearth of literature on the letter, at least in Spanish. There are two commentaries translated from English, which are not of great depth, and some brief contributions from Latin America.[7]

There is surprisingly little work done in other languages either.[8] This is probably due to the privileged place given to abstract thought in our Western societies. The reasonableness of faith is valued more than the practice of faith; the latter is seen as separate from the former, or as a product of faith's reasonableness. That is, ethics, behavior, deeds, are considered of secondary importance by our logocentric societies. Thus a letter like

that of James, which focuses its attention on the daily
practice of Christian life, is easily marginated, while the
"theological" letters of Paul are highly esteemed. It is not
unusual, moreover, that in many churches, at least the
Protestant churches, that Paul is read and quoted more
than the Gospels, which speak of the life of Jesus. In
other words, the letter is not attractive, in the eyes of
the wise.

   b. James's radical critique of the rich has contributed
to this "crafty theft" of the letter. I know of churches
where the letter is skipped over in the liturgies because
there are many rich members in the congregation, and it
is very uncomfortable to speak against them when they
are sitting in the front seats. Certain parts of James, especially chapter 5, are very concrete and thus very difficult
to "spiritualize."

   c. Certain experts have also contributed to the "interception." Dibelius, for example, compartmentalizes the
letter when he asserts its paraenetic character, that is, he
says that it is a series of moral exhortations presented
with certain characteristics. He takes this literary style
as his point of departure and then asserts that the sayings have no connection among themselves and that any
exegesis that attempts to unite them is artificial.[9] In this
way Dibelius ties the hands of the reader or exegete who
attempts to do a re-reading of the letter.

   Peter Davids says that we must go beyond Dibelius's
form criticism to discover the redactional level of the Letter of James.[10] I would add that we must place ourselves
at a certain distance from Dibelius in this regard to pro-
vide a reading meaningful for our situation today. Every
saying or tradition that James uses has its own history, as

Dibelius well demonstrates. But these sayings as used by James in relation to others clearly take on a new meaning, for they now form part of another text in another context.

Peter Davids handles the letter more freely and even tries to give it a structure and situate it historically. But in the end his assertions have little attraction for those involved with liberation concerns, for he says that it is not up to Christians to take the judgment of the rich oppressors into their own hands, but rather that God will do that at the end of time.[11]

These are just two examples among many others.

d. We must recognize that for those of us who want to read the text from the perspective of the poor, it will be difficult for us to accept passages like James 1:2, which says, "My brothers, you will always have your trials but, when they come, try to treat them as a happy privilege." We may very well decide to read a different biblical text with a more obvious meaning for liberation. By doing this we too contribute to "intercepting" the Letter of James, which we so much need to recover today in Latin America.

General Characteristics of the Letter

With regard to the date, the authorship, and the geographical origin of the letter, there is no consensus among the experts. Two recent commentaries differ markedly. Sophie Laws (1980) asserts that the author is someone who took the name of James as a pseudonym, a common practice in Jewish and Greco-Roman literature.[12] Laws situates the letter in Rome due to its similarity to other literature like 1 Peter, Clement of Rome, and Hermas.[13] Laws dates the letter between 70 and 130 C.E.

Peter Davids (1982) believes that the author was James, the brother of the Lord, and that perhaps later someone else edited the letter.[14] For Davids, the letter has its origin in Palestine. He attempts to establish its *Sitz im Leben*, which many others do not attempt. He bases his argument on the mention of farmers and merchants in the letter. He analyzes the groups that existed in Palestine before the fall of Jerusalem (45–65) and after (75–85) to help determine the period during which the letter was edited.[15]

Others with the name of James have been proposed as the author: James, the son of Alpheus, and James, the son of Zebedee. These are no longer accepted by the majority of scholars.

Egypt and Syria have been suggested as the place of origin of the letter. So, depending on the author and the origin, the dates for the letter oscillate between 40 and 130; quite a span, indeed.

The matter is quite complex and has been long debated, for the letter has very special characteristics that lend credence to a number of theories. To insist that these characteristics are a reflection of its paraenetic character does not resolve the problem.

What we can say with certainty is that the author was Jewish;[16] he knows the Hebrew Scriptures perfectly, and, keeping in mind the rabbinic tradition, we note Semitic expressions in his Greek. He was a Christian; he uses many of the sayings of Jesus and speaks of the practices of the early church (5:13–18). And finally, the author betrays significant Hellenic influence, which is seen not only in some of his commentaries, but also and especially in his manner of writing Greek as his mother tongue. According to some, the best Greek in the New Testament is found in the letter; James uses sixty-three words (*hapax legomena*) that appear nowhere else in the New Testament.[17]

Because of the controversial nature of the letter and the uncertainty with regard to author, date, and place of origin, we will leave this debate and turn to the text itself, in the light of our own context. For us the author is a man named James, who calls himself a servant of Jesus Christ. He could embody all the Jameses we know, the son of the carpenter, brother of the Lord, and great leader of the church of Jerusalem. He could also be the son of the fisherman, or a teacher (3:1), or any other. He is a person concerned about the well-being of the oppressed Christian communities and about the poor in general. What matters is not so much the true identity of this man, but rather his message for us today. When did he write the letter? At a time when there was suffering and oppression. Where did he write it? Any place in the world where the Christian communities needed it. This is one of the so-called universal, or catholic, epistles.

Proposal for a Latin American Reading of the Letter

We are going to try to recover for our people this letter abandoned and disdained by so many. It is not easy to penetrate it. Its style is very different from letters we read today. A first reading leaves us disconcerted. When

we finish, many themes come to mind, apparently un-
connected, some repeated. Because of its style, it is difficult to grasp the structure of the letter (paraenetic, with
frequent diatribe).[18] The scholars do not agree about the
structure. Many simply analyze the different themes separately, or chapter by chapter.[19] We choose to perceive a
framework, a scene, a picture.

The first reading of the letter is like the first approach
of a photographer to the subject: much is perceived and
little is perceived; there is no clarity; the image is out of
focus. So at the end of our first reading we can make
a long list of themes and important terms, but we're
not sure what we're dealing with, what is the principal theme, and other like matters that we easily recognize when we read other writings of the New Testament.
Following the order of the letter, the list will be more or
less the following:

CHAPTER 1:
   greetings
   joy, testing, tested faith
   patience, suffering, perfect works, integrity
   prayer, wisdom
   vacillation, lack of constancy
   the exalted poor, the humiliated rich
   happiness, resistance, testing, crown of life
   God does not tempt, concupiscence, sin, death
   good gift from on high
   God-Word of truth-life
   quick to listen, slow to speak, slow to anger
   anger does not serve the justice of God
   undo the evil and accept the planted word

do the word, not only hear it
perfect law of freedom
tongue, control, deception
vain religion, pure religion (to visit the orphans and
    widows and keep oneself uncontaminated by
    the world)

CHAPTER 2:
no favoritism
rich-poor, God chooses the poor
the rich oppress, they drag the poor before tribunals
    and blaspheme the name (of the Lord)
the royal Law according to the Scriptures (to love
    our neighbor as ourselves)
speak and work according to the law of liberty
judgment, mercy
faith and works together
justification by works and not by faith alone
faith without works is dead

CHAPTER 3:
do not make yourselves teachers, judgment
to sin by speaking, the tongue (examples)
wisdom, good conduct
false wisdom, true wisdom
the fruits of justice are sown in peace for those who
    assure peace

CHAPTER 4:
war, contentiousness, greed, wastefulness
prayer
friendship with God

submit to God, resist the devil
purify yourself
do not speak evil of others
judgment
the arrogance of the merchants, sin

CHAPTER 5:
weep, you rich; rotten wealth
accumulation of wealth, salaries of the workers who
    cry out
God hears the cries of the laborers
the just do not resist
patience, the coming of the Lord (example)
do not lose heart
do not complain about each other
suffering (of the prophets), Job
blessing, patience, compassionate and merciful
    Lord
no swearing (simply say yes or no)
prayer (examples)
confess to each other, the power of fervent prayer
convert the one who strays from the truth

We might note that many of the ideas are to be found in the first chapter. Nearly the entire content of the letter appears there, so it strikes us as quite dense, difficult, and even incoherent. It is presented in units that seem to be disconnected. It would seem that the only link between the units is the catchword, the final word of one saying that is repeated in the following, for example, *chairein* with *charan* (to greet–joy), *leipomenoi* with *leipetai* (lacking–lack).

In chapters 2 through 4 we see an elaboration of the themes announced in the first chapter, and one or another new theme (for example, the call to conversion in 4:7–10). At the end of the letter we note that the main themes of the first chapter are taken up again: judgment against the rich, patience, prayer, suffering, consistency between words and deeds.

The framework is still not clear. We must focus more sharply, that is, read the letter again, several times. When we see the letter more clearly, we can look at it from three angles, distinct but complementary.

The Angle of Oppression-Suffering

There is a community of believers (*adelphoi mou*) that suffers. There is a group of rich people who oppress them and drag them before the tribunals. There are peasants who are exploited, Christian and non-Christian, by the rich farmers who accumulate wealth at the expense of the workers' salaries. There is a class of merchants who lead a carefree life, with no concern for the poor.

The Angle of Hope

This community of believers needs a word of hope, of encouragement, of reassurance concerning the end of the injustice. James gives it to them from the very beginning of his letter. We see hope in his greeting, his insistence on declaring the community happy, *makarios*, in his words about God's preference for the poor, God's judgment against the oppressors, the anticipated end of the oppression, and the coming of the Lord.

The Angle of Praxis

The content of the letter is concentrated in this angle. For James the denunciation of the present situation and the announcement of hope are not sufficient. Something more is needed: praxis. He asks of these Christians a praxis in which they show a militant patience, a consistency between words, belief, and deeds, a prayer with power, an effective wisdom and an unconditional, sincere love among the members of the community.

This is the picture that I see with the eyes of an "oppressed and believing" people. This is the focus I will give to the letter.

Chapter 2

The Angle of Oppression

JAMES PRESENTS US with a picture that can be viewed from different angles. One of these is the situation of oppression experienced by James's listeners and other persons who were part of the picture. Some scholars who concentrate solely on form critical analysis point out that James simply brings together the Hebrew Bible and rabbinic tradition through sayings, proverbs, admonitions, etc.[1] They say that these are disconnected and do not necessarily have anything to do with current issues, like, for example, favoritism or judgment against the rich.

It is true that some of the sayings are used as they appear in the Hebrew Bible, especially in the Greek version, and that the ferocity with which James attacks the rich is very similar to the tone of the Psalms and the prophets. Nonetheless, this in no way means that James did not take his inspiration from the present to take the tradition, select from it, and re-read it in his own context. Sophie Laws asserts, "It seems reasonable, then,

15

to suppose that the inclusion of a teaching on rich and poor, thus creatively presented, reflects a real concern of the author himself."[2] Along the same lines, Peter Davids notes that we cannot find in the letter a clear and specific historical situation, nor a clearly defined crisis like that of 1 Corinthians or 1 Thessalonians. Nonetheless, he says, "it is hard to understand how the choice of this material could not reflect the *Sitz im Leben* of the author, his readers, or both."[3]

For us there is no doubt that oppression is one of the principal motives that compelled the author to write the letter. He made use of other materials both ancient and contemporary, phrases, sayings, familiar proverbs, but he gave them the content of the present. Each unit has its own history, as Dibelius has excellently analyzed. But I believe that each such unit, as it becomes part of another text and is articulated with other units, offers a new and relevant content. When we write a letter or a meditation, we can include passages of poetry or well-known phrases. But we give to those passages the content that we wish, or we understand them in the light of our own context, and that is how they will be understood by our readers. Preformed units, employed in another text, tell us more about the present situation of the new text than they do about the times in which they originated,[4] although they do of course maintain a close relationship with the original meaning. Thus we have before us a new and relevant letter that reflects a situation of injustice and oppression and that challenges Christians to confront that situation.

There are certain details in the picture that help us

perceive the angle of oppression. One of them is the author's insistence on recommending patience to his listeners (1:3, 5:7). This is a signal that his readers or the communities that he has in mind are undergoing difficult problems. There are other similar indicators, for example:

the twelve tribes of the dispersion;
being surrounded by all kinds of trials;
patience in suffering;
the brother in a lowly condition should glory in his
    exaltation, and the rich in his humiliation;
happy are those who endure the trial;
widows and orphans in oppression;
the rich oppress and drag the poor before the tri-
    bunals;
someone lacks food and clothing (2:15);
envy and the spirit of contentiousness, arrogance,
    lies;
war as the result of passions, pride;
we will bargain and we will gain;
the one who knows how to do good and does not
    do it commits sin;
the accumulation of wealth;
unpaid workers;
the cries of the workers are reaching the ears of the
    Lord;
condemnation and death of the just one, who does
    not resist;
have patience, strengthen your hearts because the
    coming of the Lord is near;
suffering and patience of the prophets, etc.

All these phrases interspersed throughout the letter give us hints of the problem that the communities faced. We do not know with certainty if these communities were in Rome, Egypt, Palestine, or another part of Asia Minor. But we can be sure about the experience of oppression that pervades the letter.

On the basis of the phrases in the letter we can deduce that there were two antagonistic groups: the poor and the rich, the oppressed and the oppressors. There are conflicts within the group of the oppressed. At certain points in the letter the line between oppressors and oppressed is not clear, but the implicit conflicts can be perceived. There are both Christians and non-Christians among the oppressed. And there are both Christians and non-Christians among the oppressors, especially the rich. We can also observe the experience of oppression and the mechanisms that the oppressors use.

The Oppressed

The oppressed in the Epistle of James are principally the poor. Various studies have already been published relating poverty with oppression. The poor are poor generally because they are oppressed and exploited; the oppressed are the impoverished. In the Hebrew Bible there are various Hebrew words that denote oppression, and there are also various words to designate the poor. These terms commonly appear together, thus showing the close relationship between poverty and oppression. It is not uncommon, moreover, to find the word "robbery" between both terms, as well as the word "violence."[5]

In James the relationship is clear among poverty, op-

pression, exploitation, and violence. Chapter 5 first
calls our attention to the scene we have been considering. James says, "Laborers mowed your fields, and
you cheated them — listen to the wages that you kept
back, calling out; realize that the cries of the reapers
have reached the ears of the Lord of hosts" (5:4). The
author uses the Semitic expression "listen," "behold," to
call attention to the great injustice that is being commit-
ted. Oppression, as well as holding back salaries, was
explicitly prohibited in the Hebrew Bible: "You must not
exploit or rob your neighbor. You must not keep back
the laborer's wage until next morning" (Lev. 19:13).

   The Deuteronomist also refers to this law:

> You are not to exploit the hired servant who is poor
> and destitute, whether he is one of your brothers
> or a stranger who lives in your towns. You must
> pay him his wage each day, not allowing the sun to
> set before you do, for he is poor and is anxious for
> it; otherwise he may appeal to Yahweh against you,
> and it would be a sin for you [Deut. 24:14].

The prophets continuously denounce the oppression of
the workers. Note, for example, the famous passage
from the prophet Jeremiah:

> Doom for the man who founds his palace on any-
>   thing but integrity,
> his upstairs rooms on anything but honesty,
> who makes his fellow man work for nothing,
> without paying him his wages [22:13].

There are many other texts like these. James re-reads this tradition in the light of his own context. The peasant (*ergatēs*) also lives in wretchedness because of the oppressors. The landowners could very well pay the salaries, but they hold them back. Various texts read *apesterēmenos*, which means "to rob"; others say *aphysterēmenos*, "to withhold,"[6] not in the sense of delaying, but rather of not paying at all.[7] Either text results in the same conclusion: the workers are without their salaries.

To withhold the salaries of the workers is to attack their very lives. In many cases slaves had more protection than the laborers, because the slaves could at least depend on food and shelter from their owners. The laborers, on the other hand, depended completely on their salaries. In the times of Jesus, according to Joachim Jeremias, there were more day laborers than slaves. Day laborers earned on the average a denarius, including their meal. This salary was already low, but for day laborers it was very serious not to find work or not to be paid.[8] For this reason James personifies the salary, seeing it as the very blood of the exploited workers crying out pitifully. The case was the same for the peasants. The peasants die because they pour out their strength in their work, but the fruit of their work does not come back to them. They cannot regain their strength because the rich withhold their salaries. Therefore James accuses the rich of condemning and killing the just (5:6).

The cries of the just are incoherent. In Greek literature the term *boē*, "cry," is used for the howls of wild animals.[9] In the Septuagint (LXX) it appears frequently as a protest against injustice. Recall the blood of Abel that cried out for vengeance for murder. In Exodus 2:23

the Hebrew slaves in Egypt cried out in their oppression with these same cries. The peasants, then, cry out in a heart-rending way as a sign of protest, of denunciation of the injustice. It is a cry that beseeches the Lord for vengeance.[10]

The Letter of James does not tell us if these oppressed people were Christians or not. More important for him is the experience of death suffered by the poor, who are creatures of God. And it is made very clear in the letter that God, the giver of life, hears them. We can conclude that among these poor were members of the communities that James was addressing, and that this exploitation was one of the principal reasons for their suffering. James 5:7 provides substantiation for this conclusion.

Another group of oppressed people mentioned in the letter are the widows and orphans (1:27). In the Hebrew Bible these groups continually appear as representatives of the oppressed classes. They are poor and oppressed because they have no one to defend them, nor can they defend themselves. They are truly helpless. Everyone takes advantage of them, especially those in power, like the judges, the political leaders, and the priests. In the tradition of the Hebrew Bible they are the object of the love of God and those who seek to do the will of God.[11]

Jesus is also attentive to the widows; he marveled at a poor widow who gave her two last coins (Mark 12:41–43), and he criticized the scribes who often exploited the widows (Mark 12:44). In the early church, the orphans and widows were also a major concern.[12] Interest in this class of oppressed poor was such that James defines true religion as visiting and helping them, that is, spending time with them, joining them in their oppression, and sharing basic necessities with them.[13]

The word used for oppression in this text is the Greek term *thlipsis*, commonly translated as "tribulation," "difficulty," "affliction," etc. Thomas Hanks analyzes the term as used here and in different parts of the New Testament, and he criticizes the ambiguity of the translations that hide the true and scandalous meaning of oppression and economic exploitation.[14] As for the Letter of James, Hanks asserts that his study leads to the conclusion that the translations hide in a systematic way many of the texts of the New Testament that do indeed speak of oppression.[15]

A manuscript of the seventeenth century reads in 1:27, "...protect them [referring to the needy: widows and orphans] from the world," instead of "keeping oneself uncontaminated by the world." The world as it is structured is hostile to the poor, for it keeps them out of the system constructed by the rulers and the powerful for their own benefit. James, then, urges that they be protected from the oppressive world. This variant, according to R. B. Ward, makes more sense in this passage.[16]

Another group of oppressed people that appears in the letter are those to whom the letter is addressed. Up until now James has spoken of the oppressed in general: peasants, widows and orphans, many of whom, of course, belonged to Christian communities. Thus the radical judgment against the rich and the constant call to patience. But let us look now at the communities of "the brothers and sisters" to whom the letter is addressed.

The title of the addressees is noteworthy: "the twelve tribes in the Dispersion." The phrase is much debated; only 1 Peter and James use the word "dispersion" in a greeting to Christians. Some hold that James uses the term as a symbol of the new and true Israel to address converted Jews or pagan Christians who live outside Palestine. John H. Elliott, in an interesting sociological analysis of 1 Peter, holds that this term indicates religious identity as well as a displaced and alien social condition.[17] Elliott analyzes *paroikia, paroikos, parepidēmos,* and *diaspora* as related terms connoting a community of Christians marginated by and in tension with their social neighbors because of their Christian faith.

The word *diaspora* does not refer exclusively to Jews or gentiles. The meaning of the term is figurative and implies transitoriness; it is a sociological expression and characterizes the position of Christians in the society. These were displaced persons who were currently aliens or were permanently or temporarily residing in Asia Minor. They suffered political, legal, social, and religious restrictions.

Elliott believes that the word *diaspora* in James 1:1 has the same connotation as in 1 Peter. The author of the epistle, then, employs the figure of the twelve tribes, nomadic clans, who were homeless and lived as displaced foreigners both in Egypt and Babylon. The Christians now, like the people of ancient Israel, experienced that same religious and social marginalization. Today many rely on 1 Peter to develop the idea that we live as pilgrims in this world, awaiting the next. Elliott criticizes this position, asserting that this is a sociological designation of the Christian movement and not a cosmological theology.

If we accept Elliott's proposal regarding the meaning of *diaspora*, we find in the Letter of James a community or communities of Christians or brothers (*adelphoi*) marginated or deprived of the civil, social, and political rights of the cities or regions in which they lived. Within this community of marginated people we observe different social strata: the poor, the less poor, and those who live more comfortably.

The poor were the *ptōchos*,[18] a Greek term designating those who totally lacked the means of subsistence and lived from alms; they were the beggars. The poor were also the *penēs*,[19] those who at least had a job but owned no property. Both groups were exploited by the rich and powerful, and thus the terms often function as synonyms. Curiously, the New Testament speaks more of *ptōchos*. According to Wolfgang Stegemann, the number of these increased greatly during the period of the Roman Empire; therefore, he says, "the predominant use of *ptōchos* in the New Testament must be understood also as a reflection of a social reality."[20]

In James we have these poor, *ptōchos*, present within the community,[21] for example, in 2:15: "If one of the brothers or one of the sisters is in need of clothes and has not enough food to live on...." A poor person, *ptōchos*, also appears as a visitor to the church (2:2). The widows and orphans (1:27) must be counted among the poor. Jesus calls a widow *ptōchos* (Mark 12:43). The peasant of chapter 5 would not be a poor person in the sense of *ptōchos* but rather of *penēs*, because he has a job. Nonetheless, as we have seen, many of them became *ptōchos* when they were not paid.

In James 2:6 the author clearly recognizes that the members of the communities were oppressed by the rich and taken off by force to the courts. Nevertheless, they too, or at least some of them, tended to discriminate against the poor, *ptōchos*, either because they didn't suffer the level of extreme poverty of the *ptōchos* or because, despite being in the same position as the *ptōchos*, they tended to favor the rich. James calls their attention to this favoritism and reminds them that the poor are precisely the ones who shall inherit the reign promised to those who love God (2:5).

Reading the letter from a woman's viewpoint, we are sensitive to the double oppression of women, because of both their class and their sex. It is noteworthy that James specifies the feminine sex in 2:15: "If one of the brothers [*adelphos*] or one of the sisters [*adelphē*]...," for the word "brother" was frequently used both in the singular and the plural to designate both sexes. It is very probable, then, that the needy were commonly women. Otherwise, given the patriarchal environment of the origin of the letter, the word *adelphos* would have been sufficient. Moreover, the patriarchal language is confirmed in James's use in several places of the word *anēr* instead of *anthropos* to refer to both sexes. In 1:12, for example, he says, "Happy the man...." *Anēr* corresponds strictly to the word "male," just as *gunē* corresponds to "female." *Anthropos* would be the most appropriate word in this verse, as a generic term. Due to the androcentric environment, however, the use

of the word *āner* as a synonym of *anthropos* was not
unusual.[22]

The Oppressors:
Characteristics and Mechanisms

For James the oppressors are the rich (*plousioi*). He does
not hesitate to point them out as such. His antipathy
toward them and his sympathy with the poor is un-
deniable. Interestingly enough, many of the commentaries on James dedicate long pages to the rich, thus
consciously or unconsciously attempting to relativize this
black-and-white picture that James paints. It is said that
he is simply relying on a familiar ancient tradition, or
that he is employing an apocalyptic or paraenetic style,
or that the rich are bad non-Christian Jews, or that he
is giving very general examples that have no concrete
historical reference point, or that the poor are the pious
Christians while the rich are not.

This great concentration on the rich is to be expected:
the commentaries are written in situations where there
are many rich people in the churches. How to tell these
members that according to James there is no room for
them in the church? We should note that many of the
points made in these commentaries are accurate enough;
what is striking is simply the angle of the perspective and
the special concern for the rich. A Latin American reading of the epistle, on the other hand, fixes its gaze on the
oppressed and dedicates long pages to them, their sufferings, complaints, oppression, hope, and praxis. From the
angle of oppression with which we are reading James, we
must adopt the perspective of the oppressed, which, we

believe, is that of James. And so we have first identified
the oppressed, and all our subsequent comments will be
offered from that perspective.

The rich oppressors are referred to three times and in
a totally negative manner. We see them first in 1:10–11
in a sarcastic phrase: "It is right for...the rich one to
be thankful that he has been humbled, because riches
last no longer than the flowers in the grass...." Later in
2:6b, 7, we read, "Isn't it always the rich who are against
you? Isn't it always their doing when you are dragged
before the court? Aren't they the ones who insult the
honorable name to which you have been dedicated?"
Finally, in 5:5–6 James says: "On earth you have had a
life of comfort and luxury; in the time of slaughter you
went on eating to your heart's content. It was you who
condemned the innocent and killed them; they offered
you no resistance."

The first appearance and the third occur within a
judgment. In the second the author describes the customary behavior of those of the oppressing class.

The fierce attack against the rich suggests acute problems between the social classes. James's appropriation of
the prophetic tradition of Amos, Isaiah, Jeremiah, Micah,
and others is not fortuitous. His concern for the poor
and oppressed, like that of Jesus, arises from his real-life
situation. In his study *Property and Riches in the Early
Church*, Martin Hengel describes how the exploitation by
the landowners intensified during the Hellenistic period,
after Alexander, and how the Romans and their rulers
(Herod and his successors) exploited the land, leaving
the peasants without any.[23]

At the time of Jesus, social divisions were acute both

in Palestine and the Diaspora. Joachim Jeremias describes the families of the high priests, rich and powerful, who exploited the pilgrims who came to the temple
and other members of the rural clergy.[24] When we read
about this deplorable situation we can understand why
Jesus was so hard on the powerful groups.

James follows the line of Jesus' prophetic preaching.
He does not speak of the poor in the pietistic sense common in later Judaism; nor does he follow the rabbinic
tradition of retribution, which affirmed that riches were
the blessing of God.[25] For James poverty is the result of
a scandalous act of oppression.

The rich, as James describes them, have the following
characteristics:

a. *Unlike the poor, they dress elegantly (2:2).* "Now
suppose a man comes into your synagogue, beautifully
dressed and with a gold ring on, and at the same time a
poor man comes in, in shabby clothes...."

According to Sophie Laws, the gold ring may signify
more than just ordinary wealth. It also suggests official social status, "for the gold ring was part of the in-
signia of the equestrian order, the second level of the Roman aristocracy."[26] The expression "beautifully dressed"
seems to have been the customary term to indicate very
expensive clothing.[27] This depiction of the rich man
refers to his power and wealth, whether or not he is
a Roman official.

b. *The rich are those who oppress the poor and drag them
before the courts (2:6).* James uses the Greek word *kata-
dynasteuō* for oppression. This word is frequently used
in the Septuagint and signifies oppression, exploitation
by the abuse of power.[28] The subjects of these verbs are

the rich and powerful, and the objects are the poor and weak.[29] In this case the oppressed are those of the Christian community, made up primarily of the poor. The rich oblige the poor to appear in court to extract taxes from them and legally to force them to pay their debts.

c. *Not only are the rich estranged from those who have nothing, they are anxious to acquire more and scheme to get it (4:13).* "Here is the answer for those of you who talk like this: 'Today or tomorrow, we are off to this or that town; we are going to spend a year there, trading, and make some money.'"

James criticizes these rich (although he doesn't use the term), and those who would be rich, because they think of themselves as if they were isolated individuals with no relationship to the wretchedness around them. James tells them that before they make their plans they should say, "If it is the Lord's will, we shall still be alive to do this or that" (4:15). And this should not be merely a slogan or a prayer for God's blessing on their enterprise; rather they should consider what God's will really is, whether God approves of their activities and wants them to live only for themselves. James accuses them of committing sin because they know how to do good and do not do it.

d. *They accumulate wealth (5:3).* This is the principal characteristic and motivation of oppression, as frequently described in the Hebrew Bible.[30] Jesus is also against hoarding, for this is always done at the expense of the oppressed. In such wealth is found the wages of the peasants.

e. *They live luxuriously, devoted to their pleasures (5:5).* "On earth you have had a life of comfort and luxury; in

the time of slaughter you went on eating to your heart's
content." While the rich of 4:13 plan to work and trade
to earn their wealth in a selfish way, these rich indulge in
the easy life, making others work for them to maintain
their luxuries and pleasures.

   f. *They condemn and kill the just person (5:6).* "It was
you who condemned the innocent and killed them; they
offered you no resistance." The oppressors are murderers, for they condemn to death the just person, the innocent person, the one who has done no wrong, the poor
person who has no strength to resist.

   These are the characteristics of the rich, familiar to the
prophets and to Jesus. It is no wonder James has been
called the Amos of the New Covenant.[31]

Rich Persons in the Christian Community?

We still need to discuss a final question important for
many of our churches today: Were the rich oppressors
Christians? Did they belong to James's community? For
the poor today the question is perhaps not so important,
for what they care about is that their oppression be recognized and that Jesus and James identify with them and
reject their oppression. Still we must recognize that for
many of our Protestant churches this is a concern.

   It seems that at the beginning the churches were
made up largely of poor people. Celsus refers to Christians disdainfully, alleging that the church deliberately
excluded educated people since the religion was attractive only to the foolish, dishonorable, and stupid, and
only slaves, women, and little children (*Contra Cel-
sum*, 111:53). Nevertheless, some scholars have con-

cluded that different social strata emerged within the churches.[32] In the Epistle of James the church is still made up mostly of the poor. Thomas Hanks calls it the brotherhood of the poor.[33] Other social strata, however, can be discerned. There are poor who have nothing, not even a job; they live from alms (2:15). There are others who can earn a living and have a job, but they are poor and very much exploited (5:1–6). Still others tend to look down on those who are poorer (2:6); they could be less poor or just as poor but with a value system that favors the rich. Finally it seems that there are some in the community who enjoy a more comfortable economic position, who are almost rich (4:13–17). Curiously enough, James does not call this group brothers nor does he call them rich; he simply calls them "you who talk..." (*oi legontes*). I believe that they are members of the Christian community since James reproaches them for not consulting the Lord about their plans and for not sharing what they earn with the poor.

The rich (*plousioi*) in the letter do not belong to the Christian community, or at least the author does not think they should belong to it. Of the three contexts in which they are explicitly named, in two they are clearly oppressors (2:6, 5:1–6), and in the third they are condemned to failure in all their pursuits (1:11). It is clear that this judgment is due to their oppression. It seems, then, that at this level of the early church, which began as a poor church, the Christian community began to open widely to the rich, a development that James did not look upon with favor. For him, the poor are "the more natural potential members of the community of faith."[34] In any case, faced with this growing and inevitable incorporation of high social strata,[35] James insists that the vocation of the church, its mission, is the poor, who are rich in faith and the heirs of God's reign (2:5).

Chapter 3

The Angle of Hope

We HAVE LOOKED AT THE LETTER from the angle of oppression. Now we will change our perspective and look at it from the angle of hope.

If we compare our reading of the text of James with the experience of being in a dark room, we will immediately realize that it is full of "cracks of hope," reasons for rejoicing. For the entire Bible, in the last analysis, is a proposal for rejoicing. This is not any vain joy, ephemeral, but rather a joy whose source is the proclamation of the end of oppression, the end of the corruption of human beings, who are the agents of oppression, in other words, it is the proclamation of the end of sin. The poor and oppressed rejoice because they hear the good news of a promise of liberation. Hope is the core of that experience; we hope with confidence in the promise of liberation and rejoice in anticipation. This is to have faith; this is truly to believe.

The author of the Letter of James is eager to impart this note of hope to his readers. Oppression, suffering, persecution, experiences mentioned in the letter, are not the end of human beings, nor of the Christian communities to whom James writes. He knows this very well, and therefore he emphasizes the need for hope. For only with hope are we moved to action. Hope not only keeps us afloat in oppressive situations, but it strengthens us to overcome these situations.

The details that help us to perceive the hope dimension are various: the greeting, the insistence on declaring "happy the one who..., " the phrase "consider supremely happy the one who...." Moreover, he speaks of the poor as the chosen ones, the heirs of the reign of God. He proclaims to those in a lowly condition that they are already able to rejoice in their future exaltation. He cites the Hebrew Bible passage, "God resists the proud and gives grace to the humble." And, above all, he proclaims judgment against the rich and for the oppressed and the coming of the Lord as the end of oppression. All these details suggest that one of the basic purposes of the author is to inspire hope in the suffering Christian communities and perhaps in the poor who are not members of those communities but happen to read or know of this letter.

Let us look more closely at these "cracks of hope."

The Greeting

It is worth taking a closer look at the greeting for two reasons: first, the double identification of the author, on the one hand with God and Jesus Christ, and on the other with those in the dispersion; second, the use of the Greek infinitive *chairein* for the greeting, which means literally "to have joy" or, here, "may joy be with you."[1]

The author introduces himself in a very simple way: he calls himself a servant, a slave of God and Jesus Christ. He is one who worships God and shows it by doing God's will, that is, by serving. He does not introduce himself as a great leader of the church, nor does he claim to be a relative of Jesus (if in fact the author is James "the just," the brother of the Lord). Nor does he present himself as a teacher, which he apparently was, according to 3:1. Nor does he even refer to himself as an apostle, a prestigious title that Paul uses. Rather he introduces himself very humbly: "James, servant of God and of the Lord Jesus Christ."

He addresses people who are oppressed, who suffer, as we have seen. Those of the dispersion are the Christian communities who are outcast and despised in the societies where they live. The majority are poor or very poor. So the author approaches them and attempts to identify with them, to be as they are, to be in solidarity with them. This is just as God has always done and so too God's son Jesus Christ. Curiously James refers to both — God and Jesus Christ — thus showing continuity between the Hebrew Bible and the New Testament. Such an identification with those who suffer is in itself a reason for joy.

The author uses the term *chairein* for the greeting. This is not a common term in the New Testament. Paul usually uses *eirēnē*, which means "peace," or in Hebrew *šalom*. This was the common greeting among Jews. Surprisingly James chooses the greeting usual in the Greek world, *chairein*, which, as we have said, is literally trans-

lated as "to be happy," "to be joyful."[2] Martin Dibelius
asserts that James does this intentionally, for he wants to
link *chairein* with *charan*, "joy," in the following verse,
by the similar sounds. This literary device demonstrates
the author's mastery of Greek.[3] From our hope perspective, we see beyond the literary device. From the beginning the author desires happiness, joy for those who
suffer. This "catchword," which is linked with *charan*,
a term that also means "joy," intensifies the author's
wishes to bring a word of encouragement to the communities. Thus from the very first verse we note the
joy-hope proposal that James brings to those who suffer
oppression.

The Joy that Arises from Praxis

In the Letter of James we find numerous other occur-
rences of the word "joy," "pleasure," "happiness." In
Greek the terms are *charan* (once, 1:2) and *makarios*
(three times, 1:12, 1:25, and 5:11, the last time as a verb).
In 1:2–4 the author writes:

> My brothers, you will always have your trials but,
> when they come, try to treat them as a happy privi-
> lege [*charan*]; you understand that your faith is only
> put to the test to make you patient, but patience too
> is to have its practical results so that you will be-
> come fully-developed, complete, with nothing miss-
> ing.

"Trials" here refers to the variety of oppressions and
persecutions (*poikilois*) that produce suffering, not joy.

At first glance the passage might surprise us with this paradox,[4] for only masochists rejoice in pain. But James insists on infusing courage into his readers by making them reflect on their own bitter experience. In this verse the joy is not eschatological, as Peter Davids would have it, the joy "of those expecting the intervention of God at the end of the age."[5] Nor is there any suggestion that people should rejoice in suffering per se. The author wants his readers to become conscious ("you understand...," *ginōscontes*) of the process and the result of that experience. It strengthens the spirit and forms a "militant patience," *hypomonēn* (of which we will speak in the next chapter), with fully-developed works. All this bestows integrity on the person and on the community.[6] James is really talking about heroic deeds, for, as Dibelius says, he wants to revive the heroic sentiment of the period of the Maccabees, who were oppressed by the Greeks.[7]

In 1:25 we also note joy as a result of praxis:

But the man who looks steadily at the perfect law of freedom and makes that his habit — not listening and then forgetting, but actively putting it into practice — will be happy [*makarios*] in all that he does.

The law of freedom is the law of service and is related to the "practical results" of 1:4. James refers to it as the royal law and sums it up in 2:8: "You must love your neighbor as yourself." John 13:17 says that those who wash the feet of others are happy. It is service that brings in joy. To say "will be happy" implies a certain ambigu-

ity: happiness can be a future promise or it can be integral to the fulfilling of the will of God.[8] We should consider both interpretations correct, for they are not mutually exclusive. There is joy in serving and simultaneously
the anticipated joy of the good that will come.

In James 5:10–11 we find the concrete example of the
prophets and Job who were declared happy:

> For your example, brothers, in submitting with pa-
> tience, take the prophets who spoke in the name of
> the Lord; remember it is those who had endurance
> that we say are the blessed ones. You have heard of
> the patience of Job, and understood the Lord's pur-
> pose, realizing the Lord is kind and compassionate.

The example of the prophets clearly shows us the heroism of their position; because of their deeds they suffer
oppression and martyrdom and because of those same
deeds in defense of the oppressed and the weak they are
declared blessed.

Job is an example of another kind of suffering person:
It was not acts of denunciation that caused his misery,
pain, and marginalization, but rather he suffered inno-
cently and arbitrarily. But he resisted and protested to the
Almighty, and he was vindicated. It is noteworthy that
in Job's case we see "the visible judgment of God which
consists in the happy outcome of a period of suffering
and not, as Spitta interprets it, in the reward of the next
world."[9] When James asserts that God is compassionate
and merciful, he introduces another element into the joy
experienced in praxis, namely, the participation of God
as a giver of joy. Joy in suffering is also paradoxically the

result of the practice and the grace of God. Moreover, insofar as we know and affirm that God is compassionate and merciful, our hope is greatly nourished.

Anticipated Eschatological Joy

In addition to the joy that is experienced in service, there is another kind of joy, namely, eschatological joy. This means knowing and believing that at the end of time the oppressed will be favored; therefore they rejoice in anticipation of that new order. James refers to that joy in a beatitude of the eschatological type (1:12), [10] and in his call to the downtrodden brother to glory in his exaltation (1:9–11).

Let us consider the first. James 1:12 says: "Happy the man who stands firm when trials come. He has proved himself, and will win the prize of life, the crown that the Lord has promised to those who love him." This type of beatitude used frequently by Jesus, especially in the Sermon on the Mount, describes the attitude of the one who suffers as patience, resistance, and firm hope. Nonetheless, the text does not emphasize virtue itself, but rather the promise of a new dawn, which is implicit in the initial "Happy the one who..." and in the final promise of the crown of life.[11] James, then, continues the idea begun in 1:2 ("Try to treat them as a happy privilege..."), where he says that the suffering community should reflect on the positive and incomparable aspect of this experience that strengthens the spirit. And he enforces it in 1:12 with this beatitude, recalling the promise of the Lord. The purpose of all of this is to nourish the hope of his readers. It is interesting to note that in the beginning he addresses the whole group ("my brothers"), and now he is addressing his readers at a more personal level ("happy the man [and the woman] who . . .). Hope must be real and total; it is achieved both through the community as a whole that has hope, as well as on the individual level.

The trial referred to here is related to poverty, as Sophie Laws suggests. The trial does not have to do with eschatological tribulation, but rather consists in a test linked with poverty. Laws compares this text with 2:5, which speaks of the poor as chosen heirs of the reign promised to those who love God.[12] Laws is correct: there is a parallel that we cannot ignore between "the crown of life promised to those who love him" and "the reign promised to those who love him." The latter phrase is clearly linked to the poor, and the former, which we are analyzing, occurs immediately after speaking of the poor and the rich. This relationship is not a casual one.

To have hope of winning the crown of life does not mean entering into competition and winning, to the exclusion of others.[13] Rather it means winning life itself, good, lasting, eternal, different from the past. That is why they struggle for life, resisting, enduring oppression. This is the nature of their heroism and for it they receive the crown "of life," that is, life itself. It is precisely this hope in this new life that produces joy; if they endure their oppression courageously they can be sure that the crown is theirs.

There is, nonetheless, a new dimension to this passage: love for God. The text says that God has promised the crown to those who love God. If the passage ends in this way, we would expect it to begin "happy

the one who loves the Lord for he will receive...." Or
if we wished to emphasize the difference between those
who endure the trial and those who love the Lord, we
might read, "Happy the one who endures the trial and
loves the Lord, because he will receive the crown of life."
But James did not say it in this way, and to suggest that
the final phrase responds to an interpolation or a familiar cliché does not help much. James's expression has a
meaning for us, namely, it identifies those who endure
the trial with those who love the Lord. That is, they love
the Lord; therefore they resist oppression.

Those who do not love the Lord do not endure the
trial. The loving identification with the Lord strengthens
hope and helps to overcome hostile situations. To love
God is the other part of the "royal law" that James summarizes in 2:8: "You must love your neighbor as yourself." If James does not mention the two parts of the
law together it is because for him there is a very close
relationship between the two, for as John says, if we say
that we love God and we do not love our brother, we
are liars (1 John 4:20).

Let us now consider the other eschatological joy that
we find in the Epistle of James:

> It is right for the poor brother to be proud of his high
> rank, and the rich one to be thankful that he has
> been humbled, because riches last no longer than
> the flowers in the grass; the scorching sun comes
> up, and the grass withers, the flower falls; what
> looked so beautiful now disappears. It is the same
> with the rich man; his business goes on; he himself
> perishes [1:9–11].

Strictly speaking, this is not the same joy that we saw above. James uses here the term *kauchasthō*, "boast," "be proud," in its positive sense, which also connotes an element of anticipated happiness. This is a judgment pronounced beforehand in favor of the poor and against the rich. This judgment is, of course, common in Hebrew thought. The idea of the future reversal of the present unjust order was commonplace. Mary uses this idea in the Magnificat (Luke 1:52). It is to be expected, therefore, that James, an author writing in the context of oppression, should mention it.

There is an antithetical structure between the brother in a lowly condition (*tapeinos*) and the rich (*plousios*); thus we cannot consider the humility of the brother a moral or spiritual characteristic. This is a brother who is economically poor, and he is lowly insofar as he is poor.[14] James is speaking to the poor of the Christian community (we consider it Christian because the term "brother" indicates that the poor person referred to is a believer, as most scholars agree). He tells the poor brother that he should rejoice from now on because his situation is going to change. He will no longer be humiliated but rather exalted. Interestingly enough, James does not say that he will be rich, but rather exalted, that is, raised up to the dignified level of a human person and recognized as a preferred creature of God.

The rich, on the other hand, will suffer the opposite fate; they will fail completely in their pursuits, namely, their business dealings, which are precisely the cause of their ruin since usually they are rooted in injustice and the desire for gain.[15] James is being sarcastic to the rich when he says that they should "glory" in their humiliation.[16] Later in the letter he says that they should begin to weep because of what awaits them. For now James leaves the rich no glimmer of hope: not only their wealth will perish, but also their businesses and they themselves.

The Identification of God with the Poor

If the poor and oppressed know that God is in solidarity with them, loves them, and prefers them, their hope is greater. James reminds his readers of this, although the idea was well known. The God of Jesus Christ is the same who was known through liberating deeds on behalf of Israel and the poor in Israel, and God continues to defend the poor because in God "there is no such thing as alteration" (1:17). He tells them also that if the community is suffering this is not due to God, for God "does not tempt anybody" (1:13), and from God comes "all that is good, everything that is perfect" (1:17). The persons who are the cause of this situation of injustice are led by their concupiscence to sin and become murderers (1:15). Thus some kill and others die; some suffer poverty and others live luxuriously at the expense of their victims. In this conflict "the Lord is compassionate and merciful," says James, and hears the cry of the victims. For God "resists the proud and gives grace to the lowly."

The author of the epistle is very clear about God's affection for the outcast, for he places a pagan prostitute, Rahab, on the same level as the patriarch Abraham. Rahab must have been scorned by the society of her day, for as a woman, a prostitute, and a pagan she had three strikes against her — and she would have problems today as well. Because of her hospitality to the messengers of Joshua, Rahab was justified. Although the figures of Rahab and Abraham appear together in other documents as models of faith, their juxtaposition still seems surprising. It is another indication of James's idea that there should be no favoritism in the community, for the result is always unfavorable to the poor.

The idea that there must be no favoritism within the Christian community does not imply that God is neutral or that God has no favorites. In this context God's partiality is clear: "Listen, my dear brothers: was it not those who are poor according to the world that God chose, to be rich in faith and to be the heirs to the kingdom which he promised to those who love him?" (2:5).

If favoritism is prohibited in the community it is because favoritism always favors the rich, never the poor. James forbids distinctions in this sense, not in the sense of favoring the poor, for that is what the Lord does.

The question of 2:5 is formulated in such a way that an affirmative response is expected. Thus we see that the community to which James addresses himself knows perfectly well about God's preference for the poor.

Here the poor are the *ptōchos*, those who have absolutely nothing, not even a job; they depend on alms.[17] It is not true that James is here thinking of the poor as the devout or pious, as certain rabbinic literature would have it. Many of the commentaries also follow this interpretation.[18] The context is very clear. Favoritism is being shown to the rich in a material sense, and the poor are being marginated, oppressed (*atimaō*). And it is precisely the Christians, the supposedly devout, whom James is addressing. By this I do not mean that the poor are not pious, but only that if we make the poor and the pious synonymous then real economic oppression and God's concern for this very class of people are lost. The rich become the pious poor and the poor rich in piety, and the economic order and the unjust power stay as they are. Thus the rich always come out ahead: they are rich in real life and piously poor before God and thus the heirs of God's reign.

The approach to this text taken by certain scholars is suspect. Adamson, for example, even before examining the text states, "not every rich man is doomed to be damned,...and not every poor man is sure to be saved."[19] Such an assertion would be striking even if it were made after analyzing the text; but it is even more striking that he begins his analysis with this premise. His concern for the rich and not for the poor is obvious; his readers are not of the Third World. For his part, Mitton identifies the poor with the devout and asserts that the term refers to "the class of people for whom prosperity means little since obedience to God means everything."[20] Only someone with a job, food, and shelter could affirm such a thing. The hungry, the exploited, the jobless want at least to satisfy their basic necessities, and they turn to God with those hopes.

James refers here to the poor in both a concrete way and in a general sense, not only to those who get no seat in church and are treated badly.

It is worth recalling the uniqueness of God's preference for the poor. This was unheard of and scandalous for other religions. In the Greek world, for example, there is no other god who has this preferential inclination for the poor.[21]

These poor have been chosen by God to be rich in
faith and heirs of God's reign. But James does not define
the meaning of faith in his letter, and so the crucial question becomes more complicated: What does it mean to be
rich in faith? I think that it must have a very important
meaning for the poor. To be rich in faith cannot be rele-
gated solely to a spiritual plane, completely disconnected
from their situation of poverty and suffering. To be rich
in faith includes more than being open to the Spirit with
more naturalness than the rich. It does indeed include
being more sensitive to the presence of God, but it includes something more: it means to hope in the promise
of God's reign. This is the reign inaugurated by Jesus as
he cured the sick, restored dignity to the outcast, raised
the dead. So to be rich in faith must be understood in
the same way as to be heirs of God's reign.[22] Reading
this text from the angle of hope we can imagine how
much the words must have meant for the oppressed.

This text leads us back to 1:12 ("Happy the man who
stands firm when trials come. He has proved himself,
and will win the prize of life, the crown that the Lord
has promised to those who love him."). This appears
to be a parallel expression indicating that the poor are
those who endure the test and that the crown of life is
the reign promised to those who love God. A sign of the
love of the Lord is, as we have said, the ability to resist
oppression.

Having analyzed this text in which God is partial to
the poor we might wonder about the rich. Is there hope
for them in the picture that James presents?

In James 1:10–11 there is no hope, nor is there in
chapter 5 (the judgment against them). It seems that

there is, however, in 4:1–10. In that passage the author calls them to conversion, although he does not refer explicitly to them. If we read this text separately it seems that the call is a general one, but if we read the passages as an integral part of the letter we will realize that there are various signs that the rich are the intended readers, or at least those in the community who aspire to be rich. The three most notable signs are the tone, the absence of the vocative "my brothers," and the critique of idolatry.

When James addresses the community of believers, he always does so in an amiable tone, at times even one of supplication, which reflects solidarity with those who suffer and his concern to encourage and advise them. The tone of chapter 4 is radically different, harsh, very like that of chapter 5. He does not call them "my brothers," but rather "adulterers" and "sinners." To assert that this is due to the paraenetic style is not convincing, for even though it may be, the change is so radical that we must conclude that the words are not addressed to the same persons. Compare, for example, 4:1–10 with the following verse 11 addressed to the brothers.

James uses the vocative "my brothers" to address the community. When he addresses the rich he does not use it, not even when he refers to the merchants who probably do belong to the community (4:13–17).

As for his critique of idolatry, James criticizes in this chapter those who follow the impulses of their selfish passions and become friends "of the world," which for James means being an enemy of God. Most exegetes agree that James has in mind the words of Jesus about Mammon (the god of riches) and God, that is, two mutually exclusive masters. The theme of idolatry is present, the idolatry so strongly attacked by the prophets and regularly linked with the rich and the powerful. James calls them to conversion:

> Give in to God, then; resist the devil, and he will run away from you. The nearer you go to God, the nearer he will come to you. Clean your hands, you sinners, and clear your minds, you waverers. Look at your wretched condition, and weep for it in misery; be miserable instead of laughing, gloomy instead of happy. Humble yourselves before the Lord and he will lift you up [4:7–10].

There is hope for the rich, but this is the only text in James where we see it. The condition is clear: they must be converted, that is, they must radically change their lives and purify their hands (of unjust business practices). In other words, they must cease being rich, for the rich for James are those who oppress, who exploit, and who blaspheme the name of the Lord. We must recognize that in the text of James, the rich are a stigma, just as the poor (*ptōchos*) are for an unjust society.

Judgment, the Hope of the Poor

Finally let us look at the last detail of the picture that we are considering from the angle of hope: judgment. It is not enough for James to infuse joy into the communities and remind them of the special love that God has for the poor. He wants also to assure them of the end of their oppression and suffering. He does this through judgment against the rich and proclamation of the imminent coming of the Lord. This is the strongest part of the letter. Just as the rich person, in the case of the landowner, had no mercy on the peasant, neither will James have mercy on the rich; he vents all his just fury. The style is apocalyptic; it recalls the judgment against Babylon the Great (Rome) and its magnates in the book of Revelation (chap. 17):

> Now an answer for the rich. Start crying, weep for the miseries that are coming to you. Your wealth is all rotting, your clothes are all eaten up by moths. All your gold and your silver are corroding away, and the same corrosion will be your own sentence, and eat into your body. It was a burning fire that you stored up as your treasure for the last days. Labourers mowed your fields, and you cheated them — listen to the wages that you kept back, calling out; realize that the cries of the reapers have reached the ears of the Lord of hosts. On earth you have had a life of comfort and luxury; in the time of slaughter you went on eating to your heart's content. It was you who condemned the innocent and killed them; they offered you no resistance [5:1–6].

We note how the transition from the prophetic to the apocalyptic style is made with no break, for the tone is undoubtedly prophetic in its denunciation of injustice but framed within apocalyptic judgment. The basic intention is not that the oppressed should see the suffering of the rich and rejoice in their sadistic feelings. The author wants his readers first of all to see the end of oppression. Thus this judgment against the rich is the most convincing hope for the poor. And there is no better way to express this than through the apocalyptic style. According to Horacio Lona:

> The apocalyptic style involves a hope determined by the certitude that an act of God in history will put an end to the present time and world and will bring in a new earth where the elect will enjoy salvation. This form of hope presupposes that in the present status of the world there is no possibility for salvation.[23]

Note how James simultaneously denounces injustices and announces their end. In 5:1 he calls on the rich to howl over the misfortunes that are coming upon them soon, and in 5:4, 6 explains the reason: exploitation, robbery, death. This hope for the end of oppression is not only for the members of the Christian communities, but for the oppressed workers in general. Likewise, the judgment against the rich does not specify whether they are Christian or not, although by the context of the letter it is clear that James does not consider such people to be Christians.

Later James reinforces the present hope, insisting that "the Lord's coming will be soon.... the Judge is already to be seen waiting at the gates" (5:8–9). There are other indications that for James judgment means hope for the end of oppression and the outcry of the poor. In the Bible, as José Porfirio Miranda demonstrates so well, the Last Judgment signifies the proclamation of justice for the poor and oppressed.[24]

Chapter 4

The Angle of Praxis

IN SITUATIONS OF OPPRESSION like that experienced by the communities of the Epistle of James, hope, as we have said, is fundamental. Without it life would be nearly impossible. Nonetheless, hope is not sufficient; there is also a need for praxis, deeds. James calls the communities to praxis, to make themselves felt in their environment by their testimony. For James, it seems, Christians are recognized not by their being but by their doing; by their fruits they are known. Here we will take the angle of praxis, following the lines delineated by James in his letter.

This is the sharpest angle. James writes with a heavy pen here. We can see that he is truly concerned about the life of the Christian communities. He wants them to be signs of God's reign. There are many details in the picture as seen from this angle, but they can be focused on three challenges that James makes to the communities: militant patience, integrity, and effective prayer. We can also see that the undergirding for these challenges is

51

the unconditional and sincere love among the members of the communities, and beyond. Neither patience nor integrity nor prayer make any sense if they are not motivated by love for others. Of the three challenges it is integrity that James focuses on the most. As we shall see, many of the details of the letter relate to this concern.

Militant Patience

For James one of the most important elements at the core of praxis is patience, a difficult attribute in desperate situations of oppression. Thus James insistently challenges his readers to "have patience."

Traditionally the word "patience" has been understood as signifying a passive and submissive attitude. People are patient because nothing can be done about their situations. Such an interpretation has been prejudicial for the lives of Christians and their communities, for it encourages resignation, a lack of commitment to concrete realities, and a subjection to the governing authorities (Rom. 13:1). James is not referring in any way to this kind of patience. He calls for a militant, heroic patience, one that watches for the propitious moment. There are four Greek terms for patience: *anechomai, kartereō, makrothymia,* and *hypomonē.* These are strictly military terms and are used as metaphors referring to the battles of life.[1] The author of the epistle uses two of these four Greek terms to refer to patience: *hypomonē* and *makrothymia.* Although these can be used synonymously, they have significant differences. *Hypomonē,* or the verb form *hypomeno* (used frequently in military situations), appears in the following contexts:

...you understand that your faith is only put to
the test to give you patience [*hypomonēn*], but patience [*hypomonē*] too is to have its practical results
so that you will become fully-developed, complete,
with nothing missing [1:3–4].

Happy the man who stands firm [*hypomonei*] when
trials come [1:12].

...remember it is those who had endurance [*hypo-
meinantas*] that we say are the blessed ones. You
have heard of the patience [*hypomonēn*] of Job...
[5:11].

Here to be patient means to persevere, to resist, to be
constant, unbreakable, immovable. Most scholars agree
that there is an active meaning to the term.[2] James is
very clear in this regard when he says in 1:3,4 that
patience is accompanied by perfect works.[3] This is a
militant patience that arises from the roots of oppression; it is an active, working patience. In 1:12 James
speaks of those who resist the trial and overcome it,
those who do not succumb to pain and oppression. This
is heroic suffering, as Dibelius calls it. In the book of
Maccabees, which narrates the Jewish resistance to the
Greeks, the word *hypomonē* appears more than in any
other book of the Hebrew Bible. In those accounts it
speaks of "the courage and the patience [*hypomonē*] of
the mother of the heroes and their children" (4 Macc.
1:11).

In the book of Revelation the word also continually appears with this same meaning. There the author
speaks to us of the bloody persecution of the Christians

and of the patience and endurance of the victims. According to Falkenroth and Brown, *hypomonē* frequently expresses the attribute of the person living in the light of the last days, and is linked very closely to hope.[4] In Romans 5:3 we can verify this relationship. James 5:11 alludes to the patience (*hypomonē*) of Job, a personality often very mistakenly interpreted in our time. Here we have to understand "patience" in the same sense that we have seen. The patience of Job was in no way passive.[5] Only in the early moments of his miserable life was there any indication of resignation, but from chapter 3 on all his verbal fury erupted against his situation and he did not desist until the Almighty came onto the scene. Job did not succumb to pain; on the contrary, the more he experienced attacks, isolation, and suffering, the more he was strengthened, the greater his self-confidence. Job resisted unto death and God vindicated him.

This is the kind of patience that James recommends to the Christian communities. He may well have realized the difficulty of their situation and the need for valiant perseverance, that is, militant patience. Nonetheless, at the end of his letter James employs the word *makrothymia* for patience, which can be understood as a synonym for perseverance or persistence only in 5:10–11. On the other occasions the word has a special nuance, namely, not to despair, to contain oneself, to await an event that is sure to come. The term appears in the context of the coming of the Lord and Judge.

After his furious attack against the rich in chapter 5 James continues:

Now be patient [*makrothymēsate*], brothers, until the Lord's coming. Think of a farmer: how patiently [*makrothymōn*] he waits for the precious fruit of the ground until it has had the autumn rains and the spring rains [5:7].

You too have to be patient [*makrothymēsate*]; do not lose heart, because the Lord's coming will be soon [5:8].

For your example, brothers, in submitting with patience [*makrothymias*], take the prophets who spoke in the name of the Lord [5:10].

This term for patience does not have an active meaning like the one we saw previously, but neither is it passive in the traditional negative sense. The attitude is that of awaiting, as it were, on alert. The farmers await with patience and joy the fruit that will come from the care of their plants. They can do nothing to make it come sooner, for everything takes time. So too the oppressed community of James knows that its difficult situation is going to change, that judgment has been pronounced in favor of those who suffer. It is important then that they do not despair but that they "continue to sow" and "cultivate the seedlings," which for James means that they should follow the law of freedom and live a life of integrity.[6]

The fact that James uses the word *makrothymia* for patience does not mean that we should wait for God to come and do away with the oppressor. This is Davids's position: "Patience, not resistance, is the virtue of the poor, for their hope is the parousia."[7] Rather it is a question of doing everything possible not to despair in spite of the desperate situation, relying on the future that will put an end to the sufferings.

In sum, from this angle of praxis we see that James calls the communities to have a militant, indomitable patience that awaits opportune moments.

Integrity

For James, the core of praxis is integrity, that is, consistency in hearing, seeing, believing, speaking, and doing. This is a personal integrity and a communal integrity. For James the churches should be signs of God's reign, a model different from the values of the world. At a time when there are many poor, the landowners take advantage of the workers, the merchants plot to earn more money, and the Christians are marginated and dragged before the courts, the church out of concern for self-preservation runs the risk of imitating the values of that corrupt society. Therefore James exhorts them not to show favoritism toward the rich, not to seek the important places in the church (3:1), not to be envious, jealous, argumentative, not to be hypocrites speaking badly of one another.

For James and his community, Christians should be persons of integrity, sincere, transparent, consistent in everything they do. They should be sure of themselves, resolute, decisive. The author rejects shilly-shallying, for a community with indecisive members is doomed to failure. We see in the epistle great importance placed on unity among the members of the Christian community. This is a unity that helps strengthen them to confront a situation hostile not only to them as Christians but also to other poor people who have no one to defend them. It seems that for James unity arises from integrity, and God is the model of that true unity. The integrity of the Christians is demonstrated by their spiritual practice, which is pure and untainted before God the Father if it both practices justice and does not follow the values of this world (1:27). Let us look more closely at this core of praxis.

Integrity, Fruit of Painful Experience
From the beginning of the letter James introduces and focuses on the theme of integrity. After the greeting he makes explicit the process: joy, patience, tenacity, good and complete works, and the maturity that is the result, that is, to be complete and integral:

> My brothers, you will always have your trials but, when they come, try to treat them as a happy privilege; you understand that your faith is only put to the test to make you patient, but patience too is to have its practical results so that you will become fully-developed, complete, with nothing missing [1:2–4].

In his eagerness to encourage the Christian communities James asks them to reflect on the positive side of the experience of oppression. He does not perceive the recompense for this unjust suffering at the end of time; rather it occurs now, in the heart of praxis, in the life of the communities; they experience wholeness and integrity within themselves. Paradoxically this is a humanizing process. In the very process of resisting dehumanizing forces, the communities and their members are humanized.

The experience of feeling perfect (*teleios*), which in James means complete, total, integral, should remind those who suffer that they are human beings, not things. In their experience of acute pain they should be able to integrate, within themselves, their flesh and their minds, their bodies and their souls. And because in this process the pain is almost palpable, the sensitivity of those who suffer to others who suffer is quite natural. Integralness, then, does not occur only in the body of one member of the community, but rather in the entire community, in which everyone becomes sensitive to the pain of the others within the community and outside of it. To feel what the other feels is truly a gift that should cause us to rejoice.

Integrity vs. Duplicity

James is against the two-faced person, or, as he puts it, the person living a double life. He uses the term *dipsychos* on two occasions, 1:8 and 4:8, and he gives it a negative value. This is the divided person, as distinguished from the "simple" person. The Greek *haplous* can also be translated as "open," "without ulterior motives"; the adverb *haplōs* means "unambiguously," and the adjective *haplotēs* "singleness of heart" or "pure heart."[8] In the Hebrew Bible, *dipsychos* corresponds to the phrase "with divided heart" (literally, "with heart and heart"), which appears in Ezekiel 14:3–5 referring to idolatry. The two instances where *dipsychos* appears are these:

That sort of person, in two minds [*dipsychos*], wavering between going different ways [*akatastatos*], must not expect that the Lord will give him anything [1:8].

This text refers to those who pray with vacillation, with hesitancy. James says that they are like the waves of the sea moved this way and that by the wind. Such people are a problem for the community principally because no one can trust them, because they are both with the community and not with it. Moreover they have no will power, no decisiveness. With such members of the community the battle against oppression is lost. The word "wavering," "inconstant," *akatastatos*, intensifies the voluble quality of the ambiguous person. In praxis ambiguity, fickleness, and instability are highly destructive.

Clean your hands, you sinners, and clear your minds, you waverers [*dipsychoi*] [4:8].

This exhortation is addressed to those who tend to make friends with the world, or, in other words, to follow the values of the corrupt society described by James. Scholars agree that this passage refers to idolatry: the friend of the world is the friend of Mammon, the god of wealth[9] and is therefore the enemy of God (4:4), for you cannot obey and worship two lords. Following this line of thought, 4:8 calls for integrity. These "adulterers," as James figuratively calls them, live a double life, are two-faced, are *dipsychoi*. Therefore he says that they must be purified, must clean their hearts and their hands. To clean one's hands means to cease doing evil,[10] to desist from corruption. James is probably alluding to certain members of the community who lived in a more or less comfortable situation and were driven by acquisitiveness, like the merchants in 4:13–17.

For James, then, you cannot live in ambiguity nor live two different lives. Either you believe that God generously answers prayers or God does not. Either you make friends with God or with the unjust world. Either you are in the community or you are out of it. A decisive option must be shown in praxis.

God, the Model of Integrity

James's understanding of God is closely linked to his concept of integrity. In James 1:5 God's attributes are contrasted with those of the divided (*dipsychos*) and fickle person:

> If there is any one of you who needs wisdom, he
> must ask God, who gives to all freely [*haplōs*] and
> ungrudgingly; it will be given to him.

The term to give "freely" is the translation of *haplōs*, "simply," "without second thoughts," a term opposed to *dipsychos*, as we have seen. The term *haplos* can mean "to give without reservation," "sincerely," to give of oneself generously and without hesitation.[11] For God gives disinterestedly to the needy who ask. James intentionally introduces both opposing words to indicate that we should act as God acts. This line of thought continues in 1:17:

> it is all that is good, everything that is perfect, which
> is given us from above; it comes down from the

Father of all light; with him there is no such thing
as alteration, no shadow of a change.

As in 1:5 he again alludes to what comes from God.
He employs an illustration from astronomy. God, the
father of all lights, neither changes nor is changed by
the shadow of rotation. Since God is the giver of good
things, then, God never sends evil. God is faithful to
God's own self and to God's children, born by God's
own will with the Word of Truth (1:18). God, therefore, is
a God of integrity; God is not two-faced or wavering, like
the person in 1:8. This dependability of God is insisted
on by Laws.[12]

But to know that God acts with integrity and then not
to act like God is useless. This brings to mind 2:19, 20:
"You believe in the one God — that is creditable enough,
but the demons have the same belief, and they tremble
with fear. Do realize, you senseless man, that faith without good deeds is useless."

It has been said that in this text James refers to the
classic formula for monotheism. Be that as it may, the
close link between unity and integrity is clear. God is *one*
not only because there are no other gods like God, but
because God acts consistently with the divine purpose,
which for James is the cause of the poor. The demons
are frightened by this integrity of God, for God has been
their steadfast enemy.[13] And since God does not change
(1:17), the demons tremble.

Therefore, and here we come to the core of integrity,
James challenges the communities to show their faith
through works, for only in this way is the integrity of
Christian life demonstrated. It is clear that James elab-

orates little theology in his letter and makes continuous reference to Christian practice. Nonetheless we must insist that his principal concern is not the general lifestyle of the communities, but rather, as Donato Palomino says, "the theoretical-practical unity of biblical faith for discipleship, where he contrasts the character of the militants with the structures of the system,"[14] that is, with the economic, political, and religious system of his time.

Faith and Practice, the Core of Integrity

For James, the link between the experience of oppression and eschatological hope is the practice of faith. At the end of the first chapter he summarizes the meaning of the spiritual life acceptable to God: "coming to the help of orphans and widows when they need it, and keeping oneself uncontaminated by the world" (1:27). The orphans and the widows, as we have pointed out, represent the oppressed and exploited, and the world responsible for their being oppressed represents the institutions, the structures, the value system that promote injustice or are indifferent toward it.

The Christian communities, then, must avoid accommodation to this unjust world and not fall into the trap laid by its value system. This, it seems, is what has occurred with some of the members of the community mentioned in chapter 2, which speaks against favoritism toward the rich and disrespect for the poor. Rather, the Christian communities should demonstrate the new values of justice, assisting the oppressed outcast from society.

James links practice with the law of freedom, faith, and wisdom. These three, which could be considered

in a theoretical way, are effective and alive only insofar as they are demonstrated in the practice of justice;
otherwise they are false and dead. James challenges
the community to hear the word and keep it, to con-
template the perfect law of freedom and practice it, to
speak and act consistently, as befits those who are to
be judged by the law of freedom. He is not referring
here to rites but rather to the *mišpatim*, the Laws of the
ethical tradition of Sinai. According to 2:8, the law consists in loving our neighbors as ourselves; the other com-
mandments, then, must be understood in relation to this
one.

With regard to the law of freedom, James exhorts his
readers:

But you must do what the word tells you, and not
just listen to it and deceive yourselves. To listen
to the word and not obey is like looking at your
own features in a mirror and then, after a quick
look, going off and immediately forgetting what you
looked like [1:22–24].

"Word," for James, means the perfect law of freedom
(1:25). Those who only hear the Word, without practicing it, demonstrate a lack of integrity; they deceive
themselves. If it is only heard, the Word loses its power,
because it is only in fulfilling the Word that it takes on life
and is verified as true. On the other hand, if those who
hear it practice it steadfastly, says James, the practice itself will be a cause for joy, for it is a sign of consistency,
integrity. Integrity as a cause for joy is referred to in
1:2–4.

In 2:12 James says:

Talk and behave like people who are going to be
judged by the law of freedom.

These words occur in chapter 2, where James also speaks
against the lack of respect for the poor and the adulation
of the rich. The law of freedom is a unity; you cannot
fulfill one part of it and not another. If you do not commit
adultery but do show favoritism against the poor, you
have transgressed the royal law that "you must love your
neighbor as yourself" (2:8–11). If the law of freedom is
not fulfilled in its entirety, it is not fulfilled at all. Thus
the author challenges his brothers and sisters to live with
consistency and integrity in their words and deeds; if
they have made a decision to obey the law of freedom
they should act accordingly. If God chooses the poor
to be rich in faith and heirs of God's reign, the brothers
and sisters of faith should show a preference for the poor
over the rich, rather than favoring the rich, as it seems
that some were doing in the congregations.

After the description of discrimination, James continues in chapter 2 with his concern for integrity, situat-
ing faith and works together in a complementary unity.
From a theological point of view, this is the most polem-
ical part of the letter, for he seems to be contradicting
Paul's view of justification by faith alone. In 2:24 James
says: "You see now that it is by doing something good,
and not only by believing, that a man is justified." This,
together with the example of Abraham that he uses,
leads us to believe that James knew well the expression "justification by faith." Some hold that it had be-

come a slogan and that what Paul had meant was being distorted.[15] For some, justification by faith meant having faith without a commitment to others, without works. James, then, is trying to correct this idea by introducing works as an important element in justification.

We do not know exactly what James understands by faith, but he does make it very clear what he understands by works. Throughout his letter he refers to the good works continually spoken of in the Gospels as the liberating deeds of Jesus; they are deeds that effect justice. They are the social works that the prophets demand and that are spoken of in the Sinai tradition. Paul, on the other hand, assails works related to ritual, the sacrifices and other kinds of offerings and festivities. In his struggle against the judaizers, Paul overturned the traditional thinking about the priority of these kinds of works to center on faith as the only way of salvation. At no time does he place the works of justice in opposition to justification. Rather he says they are the fruits of the spirit that are born of faith.

There is nevertheless a clear difference in the two approaches; this difference can perhaps be explained by the two different contexts. For James, faith cooperates with works, and through works faith achieves perfection (2:22). Works therefore justify together with faith (2:24). This may seem to be a heresy to Protestants, but this is what we read in James. The problem arises when we ignore the context of the passages. The intention of James, in the first instance, is not to speak about justification. He mentions this only in passing, probably because of misunderstandings of the Pauline phrase "justification by faith" (that is, if we hold that the author wrote later

than Paul and knew Paul's teaching). From our angle
of praxis we see that James wanted to emphasize the
unity between faith and works as part of the necessary
consistency in believing, hearing, saying, and doing. So
he begins his reflection with a concrete example linking
faith with the practice of justice:

> Take the case, my brothers, of someone who has
> never done a single good act but claims that he has
> faith. Will that faith save him? If one of the brothers
> or one of the sisters is in need of clothes and has
> not enough food to live on, and one of you says to
> them, 'I wish you well; keep yourself warm and eat
> plenty,' without giving them these bare necessities
> of life, then what good is that? Faith is like that:
> if good works do not go with it, it is quite dead
> [2:14–17].

As we can see, James holds to his concern for integrity,
consistency between theory and practice. What is new
in this section is the importance for justification that he
gives to "doing." For many of us this is scandalous, and
for that very reason we should study all the more James's
contribution to the doctrine of justification by faith. Like
James, we must recognize that faith without works is
dead (2:26).

Finally, James also links wisdom with works. We have
seen the Word (or the law of freedom) and faith given
life by works. Some have said that wisdom here means
the Spirit,[16] as can be seen by the fruits mentioned in
3:17. If this is the case, we can see in James a systematic
relationship between the Word, faith, and the Spirit as

elements that, together with praxis, make up true Christian life.

James links wisdom with integrity in both contexts where wisdom appears. In the first (1:5), he says that those who lack wisdom should ask for it from God. He refers to those who have not achieved complete integrity, those who lack something. The verb "to lack" (*leipō*) makes the link. Wisdom, then, is important for integrity. All the following verses, as we have seen, speak in one way or another of consistency. James speaks of wisdom in 3:13–18 as well. Here he says that there are two kinds of wisdom, that from on high and the demoniacal. They produce different fruits. So those who think they have wisdom will have to show it by their works. These will reveal if their wisdom is true or false:

> If there are any wise or learned men among you, let them show it by their good lives, with humility and wisdom in their actions. But if at heart you have the bitterness of jealousy, or a self-seeking ambition, never make any claims for yourself or cover up the truth with lies — principles of this kind are not the wisdom that comes down from above: they are only earthly, animal and devilish [3:13–15].

This text is related with 3:1, where he speaks of the problem in the community when many want to be teachers.[17] Perhaps it is these who claim to have wisdom. James insists that they show their wisdom through their good works and then it will be known if their wisdom is from on high or not. If it is, their wisdom will be pure, peacemaking, kindly and considerate, compassionate, bearing good fruits, without hypocrisy (3:17).

Integrity and Personal Honesty
In praxis personal honesty, transparency among the members of the community, is fundamental. James indicates this several times by the way he speaks. In chapter 3 he devotes considerable space to the abuses of the tongue and how difficult it is to control. Integrity is easily broken by the tongue (3:2): "We use it to bless the Lord and Father, but we also use it to curse men who are made in God's image" (3:9). James believes that this should not be the case, for both blessing and curse should not come from the same mouth (3:10). Those who consider themselves religious but do not control their tongues and so deceive their own hearts have the wrong idea of religion (1:26). On two occasions James exhorts the members of the community not to speak badly of each other and not to complain among themselves. In both cases he refers to the Judge, who can be either God or Jesus, as the only one with the right to judge (4:11–12, 5:9). For the good of the community the members should speak sincerely to one another and avoid all whispering behind each others' backs, for this wreaks destruction in the very heart of the congregation.

If the communities to which James is speaking are discriminated against and oppressed from the outside, they must strengthen themselves from within and not allow themselves to be undermined by internal divisions and misunderstandings. They must be transparent and sincere with each other. This is how we should understand 5:12: "Above all, my brothers, do not swear by heaven or by the earth, or use any oaths at all. If you mean 'yes,' you must say 'yes'; if you mean 'no,' say 'no.' Otherwise you make yourselves liable to judgement." That is, if total honesty is achieved in the community, it will not be necessary to swear, for what is said simply and without duplicity will be believed. This would mean that total personal and collective integrity had been achieved. Moreover, the community will act according to the circumstances: if someone is suffering, the community will pray; if someone rejoices, the community will sing; if someone is sick they will call the presbyters of the church to pray that the person be healed (5:13).

As we can see, integrity, in the sense of being consistent with oneself, with others, and with God, is a vital factor for praxis.

Genuine Prayer

For James prayer is a fundamental practice in the life of the Christian communities. It is mentioned several times in the letter. His insistence on the theme leads us to believe that James cannot imagine a Christian community that is not inspired by prayer, for it is through prayer that the Christian identity of these oppressed communities becomes visible. We have seen that James insists that his readers practice justice to be consistent with their faith in God. He also insists that this praxis be permeated and consolidated by a life of prayer, as an act of recognition, acceptance, and hope for the Lord.[18]

In 1:6 and 4:3 James speaks of erroneous kinds of prayer. In the first case he refers to the person who prays with a duplicitous spirit (*dipsychos*). This is the two-faced person that we spoke of in the previous section. It is impossible for this person to pray with faith because we cannot approach God with two hearts. The intimate encounter with God through prayer strips human beings and confronts them with their own selves. They experience moments of self-consciousness and self-criticism. This prayer is able to jolt and destroy the two hearts to create one heart, solid and honest.[19] Divided persons who want to pray with faith will be able to do so only insofar as they allow themselves to stand naked before God and become persons of simple hearts.

In James 4:3 he again mentions inappropriate ways of praying. James alludes to people with double hearts. They have two attitudes because deep down they look after only their own interests and not those of the needy. They bless the Lord and Father, but they also "curse men who are made in God's image" (3:9). They are not consistent with their faith; they do not know how to pray. James tells them that they must not expect that the Lord will give them anything (1:7), for "when you do pray and don't get it, it is because you have not prayed properly, you have prayed for something to indulge your own desires" (4:3).

Nevertheless, God is ready to listen to the prayers of others. In 5:4 God hears the cries of the mowers whose salaries were held back by the landowners. This is a spontaneous cry that arises from the hunger and pain of exploitation. It is a prayer that reveals the unjust inconsistency between what the landowners promised and what they actually paid. This bitter prayer is indeed heard by God; James 5:1–6 is part of the response to the workers' prayer.

Finally, and to conclude his letter, James dedicates several passages to the authentic practice of prayer. In 5:13 we see the need for prayer in situations of suffering. We should dialogue with God in situations of oppression and violence, pain and abandonment. Moments of prayer strengthen the spirit and inspire us to the practice of liberation. This prayer gives us confidence that God is present and accompanies these practices. Prayer also foresees moments of fullness in which we feel the grace of God. The experience of joy is one such moment; therefore James recommends that psalms be sung, for this will help make gratitude palpable.

James is concerned about communal prayer for the good of all. He believes that it is necessary to join the power of personal prayer to the prayer of others. Thus in situations like illness, we should rely on people who confirm the power of prayer and the certitude that the Lord restores us in every way (5:13–15). It seems that the custom was that "the elders of the church" fulfilled this function (5:14). In this joint action we see that the leaders of the early church were concerned about the well-being of the body, and not only about spirituality. Prayer, then, strengthens us in our suffering, gives fullness to our joy, and restores our bodies.

There is a concern in the letter not to give the elders the exclusive right to pray for others. In 5:16 he insists that everyone should pray for others: "So confess your sins to one another, and pray for one another, and this will cure you."[20] In the overall context of our re-reading of the letter, this passage takes on great meaning. Here the author offers advice to the oppressed and disoriented communities, some of whose members live with no consistency between their faith and their works. He advises the mutual confession of sins. This practice involves a process of self-criticism and personal and communal purification. It requires enough humility to bow our heads to let another pray for us. It means honesty and the confession of personal and collective sins, without fear, with the freedom of love. It means opening ourselves to our brothers and sisters in the same way that we open ourselves to God in silent prayer. The community that accepts this challenge will enter into the deep process of integrity to which it is invited.

The end of the letter emphasizes the power of fervent and constant prayer. James again insists that this is not the exclusive responsibility of the great leaders like the prophet Elijah, but that all the members of the community have this power. Elijah, says James, "was a human being like ourselves" (5:17), and his prayer was very powerful. In other words, the author challenges the communities to adopt the practice of prayer. Prayer will comfort them in their oppression, will exalt them in their hope, and will help them to achieve integrity in the practice of justice, as Christians faithful to God.

Chapter 5

An Open Letter to the Christian Communities

The Picture and Its Angles

WE HAVE BEEN CONSIDERING THE PICTURE that James presents to us in his letter. Our analysis has surfaced three major concerns of the author. First is the situation of oppression that provides the background for the text. It is clear that the communities are experiencing oppression, margination, and perhaps persecution (2:6). At the same time the Christians are sensitive to the poverty and oppression of others, who are perhaps not Christian. James is greatly concerned about the suffering and thus writes his letter. It is clear from the form of the epistle that James wanted to make use of the teachings of Jesus; he frequently employs Jesus' sayings although he does not directly mention the name of the Lord.

The sufferings of the oppressed hurt James so much that he does not hesitate to denounce those who oppress others and steal their salaries, nor those in the Christian community who out of weakness or opportunism become servile (2:1) or want to follow in the footsteps of the oppressors. James calls the oppressors rich (*plousioi*) and always refers to them in a negative way in the various contexts of the letter. He hurls all his fury at them in apocalyptic style. The author does not want to see the poor impoverished by the injustice of the rich any longer, and so he writes what I think can be called an open letter.

We have also viewed the picture from the angle of hope. James feels the need to uplift the spirit of the communities, to give them enthusiasm and courage. The situation of oppression and pain tends to make people feel depressed, to dehumanize them, to destroy not only their bodies but also their spirit, to make them see their oppression as normal and natural. So James writes the letter to give them hope. God has created men and women for life. So they have to lift themselves up, to resist the pain of oppression, to confront the unjust reality, which is not normal and natural. God is on their side and against the oppressors. Rejoice now, for judgment against the rich marks the hope of the end of oppression.

And finally we considered the angle of praxis. Oppression and hope are united through deeds. There is an attitude that the poor should adopt in the face of oppression. First, they must have the assurance that God is with them, and hope provides this assurance. Then they must have a militant patience, that is, of steadfastness, of resistance, of heroic endurance, all the while practicing justice. James also speaks of a patience that awaits the proper moment, as farmers await the harvest. They do not fall into despair, but rather wisely recognize the opportune moments. Prayer forms an integral part of this praxis. It shows us the close relationship we have with God in our deeds. Through prayer we ask God to act together with us in history. This is an active and powerful prayer that nourishes strength and certainty.

But James's greatest challenge to the Christian communities is integrity, consistency in all that we see, say, believe, and do. James rejects the *dipsychos*, that is, two-faced or two-hearted persons. These are the ones who are not consistent in what they believe and say, who know the law of freedom but do not follow it, who bless God and curse human beings, who belong to the community of faith but show favoritism against the poor, who ought to pay the workers' salaries but withhold them, who speak ill of others behind their backs, who see others in need but do not come to their material assistance.

For James Christians should above all show a consistency in their faith and their deeds. Their faith is alive only if it is accompanied by good works. And good works for James have to do with justice. So holiness or perfection (1:4) means being a person of integrity, wholeness, consistency. Religion pure and untainted before God is visiting and assisting the oppressed groups like widows and orphans and keeping oneself uncontaminated by the world, that is, not following the perverted values of society. Those who are friends of the world are enemies of God, for, as Jesus says, you cannot serve two masters.

The Epistle from the Underside

The Epistle of James has encountered many problems down through history. Its history is like that of documents intercepted because they fall under the suspicion of prevailing thought. James was not considered favorably because there was doubt whether he was the Apostle, the brother of the Lord. Apostolic authorship was a criterion for the inclusion of a document in the canon. He was also rejected because he does not speak enough about theology, especially Christology, as if Christian life had nothing to do with the theological task.

But the greatest objection to James, especially on the part of us Protestants, is that he overly emphasizes works, to the point that for James works collaborate in the perfection of faith, or complete faith. In these theological discussions we usually forget that the biblical writings emerge from particular historical situations. In the case of James the situation of oppression requires a praxis in the Christian communities that cannot be avoided by the formula of "justification by faith alone" — an affirmation of biblical faith that probably had been misunderstood and converted into a slogan.[1] James says no, because for him faith must show itself in justice, that is, in good works.

All these objections to James make us suspect that perhaps there is an underlying objection of a socioeconomic stripe. It would be interesting to know what the poor thought, the oppressed referred to in the letter. Did they have similar objections? It is noteworthy that in the Middle Ages there were great pilgrimages to Santiago (St. James) de Compostela in Spain. According to tradition, unproven but believed by the people, James, the brother of the Lord and the leader of the church in Jerusalem, had been in Spain. Great numbers of poor people participated in the pilgrimages, while the kings, the princes, and the rich went to Rome. Why did the poor prefer Santiago de Compostela? Could it be only because they could not afford to go on pilgrimage to Rome?

During the Reformation, the Hutterian Brethren, according to George H. Williams, based their communism on the fourth pseudo-Clementine epistle, which was supposedly addressed to James. Does this tell us something?

It is also significant that the indigenous peoples of Guatemala make more images of James than of other better known saints. Why should this be? In many places throughout Latin America there is a common expression, *"Si Dios quiere"* ("God willing"). The source of the expression is attributed to James (4:15); how did such an expression become part of popular language?

We have seen that the letter has been interfered with, but it also must have had defenders. We know of some like Carlstadt in the Reformation; he was very concerned about Luther's treatment of the letter.[2] The way the poor have read and received the letter throughout history is an important point for investigation in the future. This is, of course, a difficult task, for the poor have not written the official histories. But there are hints and these will help us rebuild this history from the underside.

The Crisis Caused by James

We said that we have "looked at" the picture painted by James, but this reading has been in no way passive. We have been engaged in an active reading of the letter because our eyes have looked at the present through the past and the past through the present. We have placed ourselves in solidarity with some persons and antagonized others. A reading in solidarity causes us simultaneously to suffer the pain and oppression of the persons mentioned in the letter, and to rejoice in the happy hopes that they experience. On the other hand, this identification is not strange. In our day the oppression has intensified. Salaries are very low and often withheld. Racial and sexual discrimination is common. Who can deny that the *ptōchos*, the poor, are many in Latin America? So our reading of James cannot and must not be passive, but rather must be militant. James challenges Christians to be authentic, to respond as they should to the grace of God who lovingly has shown us the path of God's son Jesus Christ.

Nevertheless, we must recognize that a militant reading of James will cause a crisis for many Christians today. If we cast a self-critical look at our communities we will see that we are far from the ideal community proposed by James. Many of the defects attacked by James are to be found in our churches: favoritism, competition, gossip, hypocrisy, a dearth of just deeds, contentiousness. And if we look at the social class of our members we find that there are more from the upper middle class than there are poor. The rich in our congregations often take charge, and this is a story that is regularly repeated. Per-

haps the problem — and this is difficult to deal with —
is that for the author of the epistle the natural members
of the congregation were the poor, and he excluded the
rich.

This poses a question to our rich Christian brothers
and sisters today and those who aspire to be rich. We
know that from before the time of Constantine up until
our day, the church has opened its doors to the rich and
that the rich have then taken over control of the church.
This question concerning rich Christians is very serious
and very complex. Our North American brothers and
sisters who strive to be in solidarity with Latin America regularly ask it. The gospel response of "sell what
you have and give it to the poor" is quite ingenuous today and does not respond to the structural complexity of
society.

James indeed brings on a crisis for us, a painful but
positive crisis. It is good that many poor people rejoice to
find in James a friend who brings them good news, while
others suffer a crisis of Christian identity, because James
says that to be a Christian requires the fulfillment of certain conditions. The identity crisis that James causes for
us is also a reason for joy. It can lead us to what James
calls being perfect, integral, lacking nothing (1:4). John
Wesley called this Christian perfection, or sanctification.
This is one of the greatest challenges that James, and
later Wesley, propose to us.

Appendix

Wesley and James

The Challenge of Christian Perfection

THE TIMES OF JAMES AND WESLEY and our own times are both very similar and very different. The experience of oppression and hope and the importance of praxis are alike, but our societies today are structurally much more complex. Styles of domination are much more sophisticated. False hopes abound; the ideological struggle is confronted directly. Today there is need for a praxis that takes into account the social sciences to analyze reality and act with maturity. In this light the importance of James and Wesley does not lie fundamentally in the "how" of praxis; they really do not contribute much in this regard, for their perspective is too narrow. It is up to us to fashion our own praxis. Their great contribution is rather the *emphasis* they put on praxis and the *implications of their proposals* understood in the light of our own contemporary situation.

With this in mind we can go on to analyze briefly what James and Wesley understand by perfection. I am choosing this approach because it is the closest link between the two as well as their major concern.

First, both James and Wesley place great importance on good works. This concern is manifest in both their writings. It is interesting to note that both emphasize practice in response to misunderstandings of the doctrine of justification by faith alone, misunderstandings of Paul in the case of James and of Luther in the case of Wesley.

The polemic can be detected as the background for their writings. For example, Wesley writes:

> Once more, beware of *solifidianism*: crying nothing but "believe, believe" and condemning those as *ignorant* or *legal* who speak in a more scriptural way.[1]

A little further on Wesley refers to James 2:2: faith is made perfect by works. We find the same polemic in James 2, characterized by its diatribe style.

Neither James nor Wesley denies justification by faith; rather they simply insist that faith be made manifest in its complete form, for only then can it be considered truly alive. In a manner very close to that of James, Wesley describes authentic faith:

> For that faith which bringeth not forth repentance but either evil works or no good works, is not a right, pure and living faith, but a dead and devilish one.[2]

The way that they attempt to cover the gap caused by the misunderstanding of faith and practice is the notion of perfection; Wesley calls this Christian perfection, or

sanctification. We will consider this idea in both James
and Wesley.

The Letter of James places considerable emphasis on
the idea of perfection. The word *teleios*, "perfect," appears twenty times in the entire New Testament; five
of these are in James. Moreover he uses the verb *teleō*
twice and the substantive *telos* once. The adjective *teleios*
comes from the verb *teleō*, which means "to complete,"
"to make perfect." Anything that has achieved its end is
teleios, that is, perfect or complete.[3] The texts of the letter
in which the concepts "perfect" or "perfection" appear
are as follows:

In 1:4 James says "but patience too is to have its practical results [*ergon teleion*] so that you will become fully-
developed [*teleioi*], complete, with nothing missing."
The meaning of *teleios* in this passage is "complete." The
other terms, *holoklēroi* and *en mēdeni leipomenoi*, "with
nothing missing," are explicative parallels of *teleion*.
Those who are not perfect, mature, complete are the ir-
resolute, the fickle, the two-faced (*dipsychos*).

In 1:25 James again uses the adjective *teleion*, this time
to refer to the Law, the perfect law of freedom. The use
of "perfect" here indicates that the law is complete, it
lacks nothing, and therefore it makes us completely free
if it is carried out in practice.

In 2:8 James says that the royal law should be fulfilled
completely (*teleite*), not only a part of it. If you show
favoritism, you are not fulfilling the whole law. So, in
sum, the law is perfect; it should be fulfilled in its totality,
and we achieve perfection by hearing it and practicing
it.

In 2:22 James emphasizes that faith and works form

a single unit: "There you see it: faith and deeds were working together; his faith became perfect by what he did," that is, it is complete (*eteleiōthē*).

In 3:2 James relates *teleios* with the maturity reflected in self-control: "the only man who could reach perfection would be someone who never said anything wrong — he would be able to control every part of himself."

As we can see, in James the meaning of "perfect" is whole, finished, complete, mature. He is not referring to perfection in any absolute sense. According to Schippers, when the term *teleios* is applied to ethics it does not denote the qualitative end point of human behavior, but rather the anticipation of the eschatological totality today. In the New Testament Christian life is not ideally projected as some struggle for perfection; rather it is seen eschatologically as the totality, both promised and given. In fact, *teleios* can be applied in its fullest sense only to God and Christ. When it is applied anthropologically it refers to a person who has achieved maturity, an undivided totality of personality and behavior.

For his part, Wesley felt obliged to write a book that summarized everything he had said about Christian perfection, for there were many believers opposed to this doctrine. His work is entitled *A Plain Account of Christian Perfection*. (Interestingly enough, it is criticized by José Míguez Bonino because in it Wesley injects more of a note of individualism than he does in his other writings on perfection.[4])

Wesley begins his book by describing the influence that Taylor, Kempis, and Law had upon his doctrine. He says that they convinced him, on the one hand, that there is no middle way, or part of life, to dedicate to God, but that we must give of ourselves completely. And on the other hand, they convinced him that in our acts we should show a singleness of purpose in all that we say; only through such "simplicity of intention and purity of affection" can we ascend the mountain of God. Moreover there should be a single desire governing our character. In our religious practice, says Wesley, there should be a uniform following of Christ, a complete inward and outward conformity to our Master.

All this has to do with perfection, according to Wesley. Total love of God is the motivation for all acts of those who want to be perfect. By loving God they love their neighbor as themselves. They become "clean of heart" with their only desire and purpose in life being to do God's will and not their own. Every thought that arises points toward God, and is consistent with the law of Christ. These perfect Christians are known by their fruits, keep the entire law, not a part of it, nor even most of it, but all of it. To do this is a pleasure, "a crown of joy."

Wesley specifies that this is not perfection in the sense that there are no mistakes, ignorance, or other defects, but that these Christians are perfect in the sense of being free from evil desires. These are the "developed" Christians.

He argues that if the heart is evil, it gives rise to evil desires. But if we accept Christ, he purifies our heart. Perfection is achieved insofar as we have "the mind which was in Christ" and walk "as Christ also walked." On this basis Wesley asserts that the Christian does not sin, referring to 1 John: "Anyone who lives in God, does not sin"(3:6). This assertion, I believe, was what brought on the attacks on Wesley's doctrine. It seems that some felt it threatened the doctrine of justification by faith. Thus Wesley insists on separating Justification, or New Birth, from Sanctification, or Perfection. New birth leads the convert to a dynamic process of Sanctification or Perfection. This of course is not done separately from grace, for Wesley calls them gifts or blessings that must be acquired. He uses the words "sanctification" and "perfection" interchangeably. For example, he says that the perfect man is "completely sanctified." This is paradoxical, though, since elsewhere he says that there is no perfection in this world that does not allow for continuous growth.

Once perfection is achieved this does not mean that Christians do not "fall again." So Wesley provides advice for staying firm in this process of Christian sanctification. In sum, Wesley concludes that Christian perfection is the love of God and our neighbor and means freedom from all sin. It is received by faith alone. It is constantly given; it is finally achieved only in death. In several places in his writings he condenses his thought on perfection by saying that the perfect Christians are those who have faith, love, joy, peace, and pray unceasingly, giving thanks for everything, bearing fruit in all their words and deeds. These are the Christians who are "mature in Christ."

Perhaps these contributions of Wesley would be of little significance if we did not look more deeply, taking into account his context, our own context, and the life of the churches. I believe we should thank Wesley for recovering works as part of faith. As Míguez Bonino says,

"Wesley's struggle in defense of sanctification vindicates, I think, this active dimension of the life of believers and rejects any separation of faith and love."[5] Moreover, as Runyon states, the notion of perfection in itself implies a rejection of the status quo and a tendency to change.[6] This provides the basis for rethinking this doctrine in the light of our own situation.

I think that the concept of Christian perfection in both Wesley and James is very similar, especially in that they both consider perfect those of integrity, without duplicity, consistent in their words and deeds. Nevertheless, their emphases are different. Wesley tends to relate everything to God and Christ and considers his hearers and readers as individuals. He emphasizes love of neighbor or good works as a result of total dedication to God. James, on the other hand, emphasizes more transindividual relationships in the practice and demonstration of the faith. He tends more to "bring God down into history," to implement the law of freedom in everyday life, to show the favor of God to the poor and not the favor of human beings for God. James addresses himself first of all to the community and the relationships among its members. This dimension is not absent in Wesley, as the personal dimension is not absent in James. But the emphases are different.

To return to our present situation: What does it mean to be perfect? The word itself is abrasive, perhaps because in our societies we continuously seek out perfection, but of a kind radically different from that of James and Wesley. Our contemporary value systems are backward. For people today, perfection is linked to success, competition, excelling at the expense of others. For James it is the opposite; for him it is to attend to the needy in order to be consistent with what we believe and what we read in the Bible.

Perfection in our day casts aside the poor and the weak. Perfection means having no defects. It is false because the world of appearances rules everything. In James perfection means authenticity, sincerity, while today it is appearances that matter. The models imposed by society are individualistic, having no room for solidarity. The image of perfection is provided; it means to aspire to economic success, good education, to have no physical defects, to be successful in all our activities, and to fall under no ideological suspicion. If such is the case the great majority of the poor and exploited in Latin America are at a low level, a level of imperfection, because they never will have the opportunity to reach the image of perfection projected by our society. Our churches are not exempt from this false image.[7]

James, and later Wesley, challenge us to seek another kind of perfection, authentic perfection. It is found in those who do not cause divisions among persons and communities, those who insist on integrity, completeness, wholeness, those who relate their situation to their faith and act with consistency in what they say and what they do. This is to be honest, and those who do not act in this way are dishonest. In our Christian communities we should reflect on this crucial aspect. And we should do this as well in the popular movements that attempt to transform our perverted social situation.

To be "clean of heart" means much more than to be a good person. The continuous quest for honesty today, understood in all its depth and situated at the center of our conflict-ridden history, will help us to be authentic Christians, for to be a person of integrity means to be honest with God, with our neighbor, with ourselves, and with our situation.

This is one of the greatest challenges that James presents to us today.

Notes

Chapter 1: The Intercepted Letter

1. See the discussion in James Hardy Ropes, *A Critical and Exegetical Commentary on the Epistle of St. James* (Edinburgh: T. & T. Clark Ltd., 1978); Martin Dibelius, *James*, rev. Heinrich Greeven (Philadelphia: Fortress Press, 1976); and Sophie Laws, *A Commentary on the Epistle of James* (New York: Harper & Row, 1980).

2. Wittenberg, 1522. In the preface to the second edition he omits the phrase "epistle of straw," but his opinion about the letter has not changed at all. See, Laws, *James*, p. 1; Ropes, *James*, p. 106.

3. Donald Guthrie, *New Testament Introduction* (Downer's Grove, Ill.: Inter-Varsity Press, 1970), p. 736.

4. Dibelius, *James*, p. 54.

5. The parallels with the Sermon on the Mount and other sayings of Jesus are as follows:

1:2: Joy in the midst of trials (Matt. 5:11–12);
1:4: Exhortation to perfection (Matt. 5:48);
1:5: Petition for wisdom (Matt. 7:7);
1:20: Against anger (Matt. 5:22);
1:22: Hearers and doers of the Word (Matt. 7:24);
2:10: To keep the law in its entirety (Matt. 5:19);
2:13: Blessed are the merciful (Matt. 5:7);
3:18: Blessed are the peacemakers (Matt. 5:9);
4:4: Friendship with the world as enmity toward God
    (Matt. 6:24);
4:10: Blessed are the meek (Matt 5:4);

89

4:11, 21: Against judging others (Matt. 7:1-5);
5:2ff.: Moths and worms that destroy wealth (Matt. 6:19);
5:10: The prophets as an example (Matt. 5:12);
5:12: Against oaths (Matt. 5:33-37);
1:6: To ask with faith and without hesitation (Matt. 21:21);
2:8: To love one's neighbor as the great commandment
    (Matt. 22:39);
3:1: On the desire to be called teacher (Matt. 23:8-12);
3:2: On the dangers of speech (Matt. 12:36, 37);
5:9: The divine Judge at the gate (Matt. 24:33).

We should clarify that the frequent parallel with Matthew does not imply copying but rather recollections of the oral teaching of Jesus. For his part, Davids points out the similarity with Luke. See Peter H. Davids, *The Epistle of James: A Commentary on the Greek Text* (Grand Rapids, Mich.: William B. Eerdmans, 1982), pp. 47, 48.

    6. Wittenberg, 1522. See Ropes, *James*, p. 106.

    7. William Barclay, *Santiago, I y II Pedro* (Buenos Aires: La Aurora, 1974); Eng. trans.: *The Letters of James and Peter* (Edinburgh: St. Andrews, 1958); B. Rudd, *Las epístolas generales, Santiago, I y II Pedro, I, II, y III de Juan y Judas* (El Paso, Texas: Casa Bautista de Publicaciones, 1942); Rudolf Obermüller, *Testimonio cristiano en el mundo judío* (Buenos Aires: Aurora, 1976), vol. 1; Tomás Hanks, *Opresión y pobreza* (Miami: Caribe, 1980); Eng. trans., *God So Loved the Third World: The Biblical Vocabulary of Oppression* (Maryknoll, N.Y.: Orbis Books, 1983). Donato Palomino dedicates chapter 3 of his thesis to James, especially James 5, "Paradigmas bíblicos para una pastoral obrera" (San Jose: Seminario Bíblico Latinoamericano, 1984). Julio de Santa Ana, *El desafío de los pobres a la iglesia* (San José, Costa Rica: DEI, 1985); Eng. trans.: *Good News to the Poor: The Challenge of the Poor in the History of the Church* (Maryknoll, N.Y.: Orbis Books, 1979).

    8. Apart from the classic works of Dibelius and Laws, there are few recent scholarly works on James. Most highly recommended are Cantinant, *Les epîtres de Saint Jacques et de Saint Jude* (1973); Mussner, *Der Jakobusbrief* (1964); and Peter H. Davids, *The Epistle of James: A Commentary on the Greek Text* (1982). See also Douglas J. Moo, *James* (Grand Rapids: William B. Eerdmans, 1985), and Pedrito U.

Maynard-Reid, *Poverty and Wealth in James* (Maryknoll, N.Y.: Orbis Books, 1987).

9. Dibelius, *James*.

10. Davids, *James*.

11. Ibid., p. 182.

12. Laws, *James*, p. 41.

13. Ibid., p. 25.

14. Davids, *James*, p. 22.

15. Ibid., pp. 28–34.

16. Some, especially Spitta, believe that the letter was a Jewish document and that a few Christian interpolations were made later.

17. Of these, forty-five appear in the LXX, but thirteen are completely new in the Bible (Davids, *James*, pp. 58, 59).

18. For a more detailed analysis of the style, in addition to the introductions to the commentaries of Dibelius, Ropes, and Davids, see Anselm Schultz, "Formas fundamentales de la parenesis primitiva," in *Forma y próposito del Nuevo Testamento*, ed. Josef Schreiner (Barcelona: Herder, 1973).

19. Laws, Dibelius, Ropes, Adamson, and others.

Chapter 2: The Angle of Oppression

1. For example, see Martin Dibelius, *James*, rev. Heinrich Greeven (Philadelphia: Fortress Press, 1976).

2. Sophie Laws, *A Commentary on the Epistle of James* (New York: Harper & Row, 1980), p. 9.

3. Peter Davids, *Commentary on James* (Grand Rapids, Mich.: William B. Eerdmans, 1982), p. 30.

4. Contrary to what is asserted by Davids, ibid.

5. For a more detailed study see Thomas Hanks, *God So Loved the Third World* (Maryknoll, N.Y.: Orbis Books, 1983), and Elsa Tamez, *The Bible of the Oppressed* (Maryknoll, N.Y.: Orbis Books, 1982).

6. Davids, *James*, p. 177.

7. James Adamson, *The Epistle of James* (Grand Rapids, Mich.: William B. Eerdmans, 1976), p. 186.

8. Joachim Jeremias, *Jerusalem in the Time of Jesus* (Philadelphia: Fortress, 1969) p. 111.

9. Adamson, *James*, p. 186.

10. Davids, *James*, pp. 177-178.

11. See, for example, Isa. 1:10-17; Deut. 14:29; 24:17-21; Ezek. 22:7; Zech. 7:10.

12. See Acts 6:1-6; 1 Tim. 5:3-16. See also Adamson, *James*, p. 86; Laws, *James*, p. 89; Davids, *James*, p. 103.

13. Laws, *James*, p. 89.

14. Hanks, *God So Loved the Third World*, pp. 44-50.

15. Ibid., p. 47.

16. In the *Interpreter's Dictionary of the Bible*, Supplementary Volume (Nashville: Abingdon, 1981), p. 470. This refers to the papyrus Bodmer 17 p74. See Laws, *James*, p. 90.

17. John H. Elliott, *A Home for the Homeless: A Sociological Exegesis of 1 Peter, Its Situation and Strategy* (Philadelphia: Fortress, 1981), pp. 21-58.

18. "*Ptōchos*," Kittel, *Theological Dictionary of the New Testament*, 6:885.

19. "*Penēs*," Kittel, ibid., 6:37

20. Wolfgang Stegemann, *The Gospel and the Poor* (Philadelphia: Fortress, 1984), p. 15.

21. This is not Stegemann's view; he says that there were no *ptochos* in the early Christian community; for him the community was made up of *penēs* and *penētes*.

22. For the most part James follows the LXX with this phrase. Cf. Ps. 1:1, Prov. 8:34. But in the LXX we also find the term *anthropos: makarios de anthropos...* (Job 5:17).

23. Martin Hengel, *Property and Riches in the Early Church* (Philadelphia: Fortress Press, 1974), p. 15

24. Jeremias, *Jerusalem*, pp. 95-99.

25. Apart from the tradition that is critical of riches, there is another more common tradition in later Jewish thought; in it the poor are spiritualized and the term "poor" becomes synonymous with pious. Riches are then accepted as a gift of God. James follows the former tradition.

26. Laws, *James*, p. 98.

27. Davids, *James*, p. 108.

28. Laws, *James*, p. 104.

29. Exod. 1:13; Deut. 24:7; 1 Kings 12:4; Hos. 12:8; Amos 4:1; 8:4; Mic. 2:2; Hab. 1:4; Jer. 22:3; Ezek. 18:7, 12, 16; 22:7; 45:8; 46:18.

30. Tamez, *Bible of the Oppressed*, pp. 32–33.

31. This is the term A. M. Hunter uses, as cited in Adamson, *James*, p. 20.

32. For example, Wayne Meeks analyzes the Pauline communities and concludes that they were constituted by members of different social strata, especially merchants and artisans. There were persons of some wealth but with an ambiguous social status, often because they had been slaves. See Wayne A. Meeks, *The First Urban Christians* (New Haven: Yale University Press, 1983), pp. 72–73.

33. Hanks, *God So Loved the Third World*, p. 46.

34. Laws, *James*, p. 104.

35. Hengel, *Property and Riches*, pp. 64–65.

Chapter 3: The Angle of Hope

1. James Adamson, *The Epistle of James* (Grand Rapids, Mich.: William B. Eerdmans, 1976), p. 52.

2. As documented in the papyri and other sources (Sophie Laws, *A Commentary on the Epistle of James* (New York: Harper & Row, 1980), p. 49).

3. Martin Dibelius, *James*, rev. Heinrich Greeven (Philadelphia: Fortress Press, 1976), p. 68.

4. This idea was common in the tradition of the early church. Cf. 1 Pet. 1:6–7 and Rom. 5:2–5 (Peter H. Davids, *The Epistle of James: A Commentary on the Greek Text* [Grand Rapids, Mich.: William B. Eerdmans, 1982], pp. 65–66).

5. Davids, ibid., p. 67.

6. Nor does Laws believe that there is an eschatological term to the series of James; for Laws the trials lead to personal integrity, an end in itself (*James*, p. 52).

7. Dibelius, *James*, p. 73.

8. Davids asserts that this is an eschatological saying (*James*, p. 100). Sophie Laws recognizes the ambiguity and thinks that it is probable that the author considers both interpretations to be correct (*James*, pp. 87–88).

9. Dibelius, *James*, p. 246.

10. According to Klaus Koch there are two types of beatitudes in the Bible: one appears in the wisdom literature of the Old Testament as the conclusion to a series of prayers or a logical argument, and the other is the apocalyptic blessing directed to those who will be saved in the last judgment and participate in the new world because they have remained true to their faith. The blessing of James falls in the latter category (*The Growth of the Biblical Tradition* [New York: Charles Scribner's Sons, 1969], p. 7).

11. Ibid., p. 8.

12. Laws, *James*, p. 67.

13. Adamson, *James*, p. 67.

14. Laws, *James*, p. 62.

15. See Elsa Tamez, *The Bible of the Oppressed* (Maryknoll, N.Y.: Orbis Books, 1982), pp. 49–50.

16. This is the view of Dibelius and Laws, as opposed to others like Ropes and Adamson, who believe that the rich person referred to is a member of the Christian community because the word *adelphos*, they hold, refers to both the poor man and the rich man.

17. Kittel, *Theological Dictionary of the New Testament*, 6:888.

18. Dibelius, Adamson, Davids, Mitton, etc.

19. Adamson, *James*, pp. 108–109.

20. Leslie Mitton, *The Epistle of James* (Grand Rapids, Mich.: William B. Eerdmans, 1966), p. 86.

21. Kittel, 6:887.

22. This is also the view of Davids, *James*, pp. 111, 112.

23. Horacio Lona, "L'attente et savoir de la fin apocalyptique et eschatologique neotestamentaires," *Lumière et Vie*, no. 160, p. 27.

24. José Porfirio Miranda, *Marx and the Bible* (Maryknoll, N.Y.: Orbis Books, 1974), pp. 111–136.

Chapter 4: The Angle of Praxis

1. Colin Brown, *Dictionary of New Testament Theology* (Grand Rapids, Mich.: Zondervan, 1977), 2:764.

2. See Dibelius, Laws, Adamson, Davids, etc.

3. The term "perfect works" has been translated as "the patience that reaches perfection."

4. In Brown, *Dictionary,* p. 774.

5. I do not agree with scholars who hold that James had in mind the Job of the *Testament of Job* and not the canonical book of Job. The Job of the *Testament* is patient in the sense of passive resignation.

6. The term *makrothymia* has another meaning, even more common in the LXX and in other parts of the New Testament. In the Greek Old Testament it is used to refer to the patience of God. God is patient with human beings; God mercifully controls the divine anger to give human beings time to be converted and change their attitudes. In this case to have patience is to have mercy, to have clemency. In Rom. 2:4 the patience of God leads us to conversion — *metanoia*. In the parable of the unjust steward, Matt. 26, this meaning is clearly seen. The steward asked for patience from the Lord (*makrothymia*) for his debt and promised to pay back everything. In his mercy the master pardoned the debt, which the steward did not do with his peers, and so ended up in jail. This connotation does not easily fit into our text of James, for the author indicates the meaning we should use with his example of the laborer.

7. Peter H. Davids, *The Epistle of James: A Commentary on the Greek Text* (Grand Rapids, Mich.: William B. Eerdmans, 1982), p. 181.

8. Kittel, *Theological Dictionary of the New Testament,* 1:386–387.

9. James Adamson, *The Epistle of James* (Grand Rapids, Mich.: William B. Eerdmans, 1976), p. 170.

10. Davids, *James,* p. 167.

11. Kittel, 1:386–387.

12. Sophie Laws, *A Commentary on the Epistle of James* (New York: Harper & Row, 1980), Laws, pp. 49–61, 126.

13. Ibid., p. 126.

14. In his unpublished dissertation, "Paradigmas bíblicos para una pastoral obrera" (San José, Costa Rica: Seminario Bíblico Latinoamericano, 1984), p. 145.

15. Laws, *James,* p. 131.

16. See J. A. Kirk, "The Meaning of Wisdom in James: Examination of a Hypothesis," *New Testament Studies,* vol. 16, no. 1 (October 1969), pp. 24–38.

17. See Davids, *James,* p. 149; cf. Dibelius, *James,* p. 208.

18. Jon Sobrino speaks of "the necessity of prayer for discovering

the meaning of Christian praxis within this praxis" (*La oración de Jesús y del cristiano* [Mexico City: CRT, 1981], p. 8).

19. Frei Betto believes that "prayer makes us more sensitive to the manifestations of institutionalized lies" (*Oração na ação* [Rio de Janeiro: Civilização Brasileira, 1977], p. 38).

20. It seems that James intentionally did not assign the elders the exclusive right to pray for others. This text and the example of Elijah suggest this.

Chapter 5: An Open Letter to the Christian Communities

1. Sophie Laws, *A Commentary on the Epistle of James* (New York: Harper & Row, 1980), p. 131

2. George H. Williams, *La Reforma radical* (Mexico City: Fondo de Cultura Económica, 1983), p. 468; in Eng. see *Radical Reformation* (Philadelphia: Westminster, 1962).

Appendix: Wesley and James

1. John Wesley, "A Plain Account of Christian Perfection," in Frank Whaling, ed., *John and Charles Wesley: Selected Prayers, Hymns, Journal Notes, Sermons, Letters and Treatises,* The Classics of Western Spirituality (New York: Paulist Press, 1981), p. 363.

2. "Of True Christian Faith," in Albert C. Outler, ed., *John Wesley, A Library of Protestant Thought* (New York: Oxford University Press, 1964), p. 128.

3. R. Schippers, "Goal," in *Dictionary of New Testament Theology,* ed. Colin Brown (Grand Rapids, Mich.: Zondervan, 1976), 2:59.

4. Ibid., p. 65

5. José Míguez Bonino, "Justificación, santificación, y plenitud," in *La tradición protestante en la teología latinoamericana,* ed. José Duque (San José, Costa Rica: DEI, 1983), p. 254.

6. Ibid., p. 250.

7. Theodore Runyon, "Wesley and the Theologies of Liberation," in *Sanctification and Liberation,* ed. Theodore Runyon (Nashville: Abingdon, 1981).

Bibliography

Adamson, James B. *The Epistle of James*. New International Commentary on the New Testament. Grand Rapids, Mich.: William B. Eerdmans Publishing Co., 1976.

Betto, Frei. *Oração na ação*. Rio de Janeiro: Ed. Civilização Brasileira, S.A., 1977.

Brown, Colin. *Dictionary of New Testament Theology.* Grand Rapids, Mich.: Zondervan, 1977.

Davids, Peter H. *The Epistle of James: A Commentary on the Greek Text.* The New International Greek Testament Commentary. Grand Rapids, Mich.: William B. Eerdmans Publishing Co., 1982.

de Santa Ana, Julio. *Good News to the Poor: The Challenge of the Poor in the History of the Church.* Maryknoll, N.Y.: Orbis Books, 1979.

Dibelius, Martin. *James.* Revised by Heinrich Greeven. Hermeneia. Philadelphia: Fortress, 1976.

Elliott, John H. *A Home for the Homeless: A Sociological Exegesis of 1 Peter, Its Situation and Strategy.* Philadelphia: Fortress, 1981.

Guthrie, Donald. *New Testament Introduction.* Downers Grove, Ill.: Inter-Varsity Press, 1970.

Hanks, Thomas. *God So Loved the Third World: The Biblical Vocabulary of Oppression.* Maryknoll, N.Y.: Orbis Books, 1983.

Hengel, Martin. *Property and Riches in the Early Church: Aspects of a Social History of Early Christianity.* Philadelphia: Fortress Press, 1974.

The Interpreter's Dictionary of the Bible, Supplementary Volume. Nashville: Abingdon, 1981.

Jeremias, Joachim. *Jerusalem in the Time of Jesus: An Investigation into Economic and Social Conditions during the New Testament Period.* Philadelphia: Fortress, 1969.

Kirk, J. A. "The Meaning of Wisdom in James: Examination of a Hypothesis," in *New Testament Studies,* vol. 16, no. 1 (October 1969), pp. 24–38.

Koch, Klaus. *The Growth of the Biblical Tradition: The Form-Critical Method.* New York: Charles Scribner's Sons, 1969.

Laws, Sophie. *The Epistle of James.* New York: Harper & Row Publishers, 1980.

Lona, Horacio. "L'attente et savoir de la fin apocalyptique et eschatololologie neotestamentaires" in *Lumière et Vie,* no. 160, p. 27.

Meeks, Wayne. *The First Urban Christians: The Social World of the Apostle Paul.* New Haven, Conn.: Yale University Press, 1983.

Míguez Bonino, José. "Justificación, Santificación y Plenitud" in *La tradición protestante en la teología latinoamericana.* Ed. José Duque. San José, Costa Rica: DEI, 1983.

Mitton, Leslie. *The Epistle of James.* Michigan: William B. Eerdmans Publishing Co., 1966.

Miranda, José Porfirio. *Marx and the Bible: A Critique of the Philosophy of Oppression.* Maryknoll, N.Y.: Orbis Books, 1974.

Palomino, Donato. "Paradigmas bíblicos para una pastoral obrera," Seminario Bíblico Latinoamericano, 1984.

Ropes, James Hardy. *A Critical and Exegetical Commentary on the Epistle of James.* International Critical Commentary. Edinburgh: T. & T. Clark Ltd., 1916.

Runyon, Theodore. "Wesley and the Theologies of Liberation" in *Sanctification & Liberation.* Ed. Theodore Runyon. Nashville: Abingdon, 1981.

Schippers, R. "Goal", in *Dictionary of the New Testament Theology.* Ed. Colin Brown, Grand Rapids, Mich.: Zondervan, 1976, vol. 2., p. 59.

Schreiner, Josef. *Forma y propósito del Nuevo Testamento.* Barcelona: Herder, 1973.

Sobrino, Jon. *La oración de Jesús y del cristiano.* Mexico City: CRT, 1981.

Stegemann, Wolfgang. *The Gospel and the Poor.* Philadelphia: Fortress, 1984.

Tamez, Elsa. *Bible of the Oppressed.* Maryknoll, N.Y.: Orbis Books, 1982.

Wesley, John. "A Plain Account of Christian Perfection." In Frank Whaling, ed. *John and Charles Wesley: Selected Prayers, Hymns, Journal Notes, Sermons, Letters and Treatises.* The Classics of Western Spirituality. New York: Paulist Press, 1981.

Wesley, John. "Of True Christian Faith." In Albert C. Outler, ed. *John Wesley.* A Library of Protestant Thought. New York: Oxford University Press, 1964.

Williams, George H. *Radical Reformation.* Philadelphia: Westminster, 1962; Span. trans.: *La Reforma radical.* Mexico City: Fondo de Cultura Económica, 1983.

Index of Scriptural References

Index of Authors

Comments on
The Scandalous Message of James ...

"Tamez provides profound theological insights regarding James's teachings on faith and works, the poor and the rich, and how Christians are to live. This book was written and translated with a clarity that makes it a pleasure to read."

Otto Spehr, translator, Kpelle New Testament

"*The Scandalous Message of James* will make a useful Bible study guide for lay and pastoral groups in the U.S. that desire the correction of a global encounter with the gospel. Liberation hermeneutic is rapidly broadening its scope from its focus on Exodus and Luke 4 to the whole of Scripture. Elsa Tamez's rereading of James is a daring and useful result of this shift.

"She teaches us to read the Bible from angles unlike those familiar to conventional Bible study. To read the book of James from the angles of oppression, hope, and praxis enriches the interpretation beyond ordinary expositions. This reading will cause a crisis for rich Christians today — and for those who aspire to be rich. This crisis is both painful and positive because it calls us to conversion — a conversion of global dimensions.

"Latin American Methodists are reclaiming the Wesleyan teaching on sanctification. Elsa Tamez is among those who see sanctification as the resolution of the faith/works debate. She compares Wesley and James on their definitions of holiness, in the light of today's social-political-economic context. Thus she offers a theology of sanctification that is a gift of Latin American Wesleyanism to ecumenical faith."

Dow Kirkpatrick, United Methodist pastor and Latin American missionary-in-reverse, editor of *Faith Born in the Struggle for Life: A Rereading of Protestant Faith in Latin America Today*

"Those who think 'God's option for the poor' is just a contemporary slogan will be surprised to find this option at the heart of the epistle of James. This is the 'scandalous message' that Elsa Tamez's hermeneutic of suspicion reveals to us. Writing from the perspective of the poor, she uses careful and clearly written analysis to portray James's message that oppression and hope are united through deeds."

Letty Russell, Professor of Theology, The Divinity School, Yale University